For Israel

warm wishes c [P9-ELP-192]

Erich

Katrina

David

Breaking the Logjam

Breaking the Logjam

Environmental Protection That Will Work

David Schoenbrod, Richard B. Stewart,
Katrina M. Wyman

Illustrations by Deborah Paulus-Jagrič

Yale University Press   *New Haven & London*

Published with assistance from the foundation established in memory of
Calvin Chapin of the Class of 1788, Yale College.

Designed by James J. Johnson and set in Photina Roman type by Keystone
Typesetting, Inc., Orwigsburg, Pennsylvania.
Printed in the United States of America by Sheridan Books.

Library of Congress Cataloging-in-Publication Data

Schoenbrod, David.
    Breaking the logjam : environmental protection that will work /
David Schoenbrod, Richard B. Stewart, Katrina M. Wyman;
illustrations by Deborah Paulus-Jagrič.
        p. cm.
    Includes bibliographical references and index.
    ISBN 978-0-300-14960-9 (hardcover : alk. paper)
        1. Environmental law—United States. 2. Law reform—United States.
I. Stewart, Richard B. II. Wyman, Katrina M., 1970– III. Title.
KF3775.S365 2010
344.7304′6—dc22
2009034627

A catalogue record for this book is available from the British Library.

This paper meets the requirements of ANSI/NISO Z39.48–1992 (Permanence
of Paper).

10   9   8   7   6   5   4   3   2   1

To the pioneers of modern environmental protection

At some time in the future—probably when this current version of gridlock is more apparent—we will be able to deal seriously with the reform we all recognize is needed. What would that reform look like?

—William D. Ruckelshaus, 1995

Contents

Preface
The Logjammed Congress

Environmental protection in the United States is increasingly stuck after several decades of significant but patchy and incomplete success. The shortcomings cannot be pinned entirely, or even primarily, on presidents getting too cozy with special interests. Multiple administrations under presidents of both parties have fallen well short of the goals of the environmental statutes. The statutes themselves are at the root of the problem.

Legislation enacted by Congress in the 1970s governs how we manage the environment today in the twenty-first century. These statutes require federal agencies to, in effect, dictate most of the who, where, what, and how of environmental protection. This centralized, highly prescriptive technique achieved hefty cuts in pollution from large factories, new cars, and other major sources but cannot wring much more from them without far greater cost and difficulty. It has not been very successful in dealing with small sources, the conduct of millions of individuals, and crosscutting environmental problems. The low-hanging fruit has been picked.

Moreover, since the 1970s, the environmental challenge has become tougher. As the easier problems have been solved, the problems that the old statutes cannot solve have grown in relative importance. To this backlog are added newer problems such as climate change and ocean degradation, which are also, for the most part, beyond the old statutes' prescriptive technique.

The old statutes give agencies duties too complicated to fulfill and require them to use methods more burdensome than necessary to achieve environmental goals. In the end the burdens fall on consumers and other voters. They resist and agencies get paralyzed. The ill will generated sours the ground for statutory revisions needed to address the newer problems and adopt better methods for dealing with old ones.

The growing obsolescence of our environmental statutes has become particularly troubling with the heightened urgency of climate change and the crisis in the economy. Inflexible and wasteful ways of achieving vital environmental goals deter action and encumber our productive energies.

This book shows how to move forward. Reformed statutes that make greater use of economic incentives and other more flexible regulatory tools would save on costs, prompt technological innovations that would pay dividends for the environment and economy, and give agencies doable jobs. Such statutes would work with, rather than against, new programs to stimulate the economy and encourage green technology.

The old statutes were the best response to the environmental challenge as it was understood in the early 1970s—the dawn of the modern environmental era. Today, however, the challenge is different and we know more. Past success and new science have generated an ecological succession in environmental protection that calls for new tools. Although government should still employ top-down prescriptive regulation in some cases, it should increasingly employ other regulatory tools that set mandatory goals but allow private and public actors leeway in how to achieve them. These tools include more flexible market-based regulations that penalize failure to move in the right direction and reward success, particularly success in developing innovative ways to be green;

that employ property right-like instruments in natural resources as a regulatory strategy; and that require the disclosure of information as a tactic to energize consumers, investors, and citizen activists as well as prod managers and regulators.

Unfortunately, however, Congress has generally failed to reform the statutes to meet modern needs. This failure has spanned decades. Partisanship discouraged cooperation in the 1980s, and the rancor solidified into a legislative logjam that has persisted since 1990. Congress and the president produced next to no major environmental legislation during the last half of the presidency of George H. W. Bush, the two terms of William J. Clinton, and the two terms of George W. Bush. Thus, although environmental experts have long discussed the need for modernizing the regulatory toolbox, Congress, together with successive administrations, has largely failed to respond.

There is hope, nonetheless, of breaking the logjam in Congress. The public demands action on climate change, the dominant environmental problem, and government cannot act effectively and efficiently without new legislation. There is a broad consensus in Congress that any climate-change legislation must use tools not generally available under the old statutes.

The work of Congress and the administration cannot, and should not, stop with climate change. Because climate change and the control of conventional air pollution are inextricably related, Congress must overhaul the Clean Air Act. Beyond that, the same logic that calls for using better tools on climate change supports revising other old statutes to allow their use on other environmental problems. The presidential candidates of both major parties in 2008, John McCain and Barack Obama, suggested as much.

Climate change adds urgency to reforming these old statutes. It exacerbates the environmental problems to which they are addressed, such as species extinction and water pollution. We must make these old statutes more effective and efficient. Congress cannot in good faith ask voters to bear the costs of curbing climate change without updating the statutes to eliminate unnecessary burdens in achieving established as well as new environmental objectives and making them more effective in actually achieving them.

What is needed but has been lacking is a blueprint for reforming the basic structure of federal environmental statutes other than with specific regard to climate change. In 2006 we launched "Breaking the Logjam: Environmental Reform for the New Congress and Administration," a joint undertaking of New York Law School and New York University School of Law. It undertook the work needed to provide Congress and the president who would take office in 2009 with concrete proposals for wide-ranging reforms in federal environmental statutes.

We set out to develop proposals for statutory reform in light of four principles. The first is to adopt better tools whenever they can reliably achieve environmental goals. This principle is the most fundamental because it helps achieve the other three. The second is to realign the responsibilities of the federal government and the states so that each level has more effective power over the environmental problems it is best placed to address. The third is to face trade-offs openly and based on reliable information. The fourth is to use crosscutting regulatory approaches that address underlying causes. These principles have won acceptance from many experts of the left and right, though there are points of disagreement.

These principles are not new to scholars, but the scholarship has generally discussed them separately and in the abstract. What is new is to develop concrete proposals that apply these four principles in combination to a wide array of environmental problems. That is what we set out to do.

We began by enlisting environmental experts with a broad range of specialties and viewpoints to draft proposals and critique them. Drawing upon the experience and judgment of a diverse and prominent group of experts would give the undertaking credibility. Here our own long and varied experiences in environmental protection helped. One of us began working on environmental justice issues in 1969 at the antipoverty organization that Senator Robert Kennedy established in Bedford-Stuyvesant. Another joined the board of the Environmental Defense Fund in 1976. Our collective experience includes important roles at the Environmental Defense Fund and the Natural Resources Defense Council, a high-level environmental appointment under President George H. W. Bush, and positions with the Cato Institute, the American Enterprise Institute, and the Health Effects Institute. Drawing upon individuals who are veterans from all sides of environmental conflicts and who represent diverse perspectives within the academy, we enlisted more than fifty experts from around the country (identified at the end of this preface) to write proposals or to comment upon them or the project as the whole. We included individuals who had points of disagreement with our approach and those of others in order to subject the proposals to robust scrutiny.

Some experts were asked to present proposals on particular policy areas such as climate, oceans, air pollution, water pollution, farm policy, grazing on the public lands, federal water policy, and other timely issues. Others were asked to present proposals on crosscutting topics such as improving regulatory science and the application of cost-benefit analysis to environmental regulation.

Many presented early drafts to a seminar at New York University School of Law in the fall of 2007. Then, most of the experts came together for a symposium at NYU on March 28 and 29, 2008, where they presented new drafts of their proposals to each other and an audience of approximately 250 people, which included other experts from national, state, and local environmental advocacy groups, major corporations, governments at all levels, think tanks, and academia.

The proposals, refined on the basis of the discussion at the symposium, were published in a special 1,061-page issue of the *New York University Environmental Law Journal* at the beginning of 2009. The proposals add up to a comprehensive vision for a new generation of federal environmental statutes. With this work as the foundation, we as leaders of the project developed our own set of recommendations. They are summarized in a report published by New York Law School, which was released to members of the newly elected Congress and administration soon after they took office in 2009. (The law journal essays, the report, and an annex to the report that goes into greater detail on climate change and air pollution are available at www.breakingthelogjam.org.) Work continued at a seminar at New York Law School in the spring of 2009.

We have discussed our proposals with veteran congressional staff from both sides of the aisle. Although they differ on how high to set our environmental goals, they saw much sense in our suggestions on how to structure the nation's efforts to achieve whatever goals are set. Nonetheless, they believe that our proposals will not become a reality unless opinion leaders and the informed public understand that our statutes have grown obsolete and must be updated. That is where this book comes in. It tells nonspecialists of core problems in the statutes and explains why Congress, teamed with administrative leadership, can and must fix them. It is not a compendium of the proposals detailed in the law journal and summarized in the report. Rather, this book is a call for action through public understanding.

We are deeply indebted to the project participants, listed below, but we bear sole responsibility for the recommendations in the project report and this book.

Kate Adams, Vice President and General Counsel of Honeywell Specialty Materials.

Jonathan H. Adler, Professor of Law and Director of the Center for Business Law & Regulation at Case Western Reserve University School of Law.

Geoff Anderson, President and CEO of Smart Growth America.

Kai S. Anderson, Senior Vice President of Cassidy & Associates, a Washington, D.C., consulting firm.

John S. Applegate, Executive Associate Dean for Academic Affairs and

Walter W. Foskett Professor of Law at the Indiana University School of
Law–Bloomington, and Vice President for Planning and Policy at Indiana
University.

Chang-Hee Christine Bae, Associate Professor in the Department of Urban
Design and Planning at the University of Washington, Seattle.

Michael Bean, Counselor to Tom Strickland, Assistant Secretary of Interior
for Fish, Wildlife, and Parks.

David T. Buente, Jr., Head of Sidley Austin's environmental group.

Marcia Dystryn, Executive Director of the New York League of Conservation Voters, a statewide environmental advocacy organization.

Jonathan Z. Cannon, Professor and Director of the Environmental and Land
Use Law Program at the University of Virginia School of Law.

Leslie Carothers, President of the Environmental Law Institute.

Cary Coglianese, Deputy Dean and Edward B. Shils Professor of Law and
Professor of Political Science at the University of Pennsylvania and Director of the Penn Program on Regulation.

Robert Crandall, Senior Fellow in the Economic Studies Program of the
Brookings Institution and a founder of Criterion Economics, a Washington, D.C., consulting firm.

Joshua Eagle, Assistant Professor of Law at the University of South Carolina School of Law.

E. Donald Elliott, Chair of the Environmental, Health and Safety Department of Willkie Farr & Gallagher LLP and Adjunct Professor at Yale and
Georgetown Law Schools.

Daniel C. Esty, Hillhouse Professor of Environmental Law and Policy at
Yale University, with appointments in the Environment and Law Schools,
and Director of the Center for Business and the Environment at Yale and
the Yale Center for Environmental Law and Policy.

David H. Festa, Vice President, West Coast Operations, Environmental Defense Fund.

Peter Gordon, Professor at University of Southern California's School of
Policy, Planning and Development.

Carol Casazza Herman, Project Counsel, Breaking the Logjam Project.

James L. Huffman, Erskine Wood Sr. Professor of Law at Lewis and Clark Law School in Portland, Oregon.

Lawrence S. Huntington, Chairman of the Woods Hole Research Center.

Brian D. Israel, Partner in the Washington, D.C., office of Arnold & Porter LLP.

David Johnson, Visiting Professor of Law at New York Law School and Senior Fellow, Center for Democracy and Technology.

Bradley C. Karkkainen, Professor of Law and Henry J. Fletcher Chair at the University of Minnesota Law School and a Founding Fellow of the University's interdisciplinary Institute on the Environment.

Nathaniel Keohane, Director of Economic Policy and Analysis at the Environmental Defense Fund.

Jee Mee Kim, Vice President and Director of Planning at Sam Schwartz Engineering.

Richard Lazarus, Professor of Law and Faculty Director of the Supreme Court Institute at the Georgetown University Law Center.

Peter Lehner, Executive Director of the Natural Resources Defense Council and Adjunct Professor of Environmental Law at Columbia Law School.

John Leshy, Harry D. Sunderland Distinguished Professor of Law at the University of California Hastings College of the Law and Vice-Chair of the Board of the Wyss Foundation.

Michael A. Livermore, Executive Director of the Institute for Policy Integrity at New York University School of Law.

Angus Macbeth, senior counsel at Sidley Austin, where he served as head of its environmental law practice for eleven years.

Gary Marchant, Lincoln Professor of Emerging Technologies, Law, and Ethics at the Sandra Day O'Connor College of Law and Director of the Center for the Study of Law, Science, and Technology at Arizona State University.

Felicia Marcus, Western Director, Natural Resources Defense Council.

Molly S. McUsic, Executive Director of the Wyss Foundation.

G. Tracy Mehan III, principal, The Cadmus Group, Inc., an environmental consulting firm.

Andrew P. Morriss, H. Ross and Helen Workman Professor of Law and Professor of Business at the University of Illinois and Professor in the Institute for Government and Public Affairs.

Beth Noveck, Professor of Law and Director of the Institute for Information Law and Policy at New York Law School and United States Deputy Chief Technology Officer for Open Government in the Executive Office of the President .

Deborah Paulus-Jagrič, Educational Services Reference Librarian at New York University School of Law.

William F. Pedersen, Counsel in the Environmental and Natural Resources practice of Perkins Coie.

Paul R. Portney, Dean of the Eller College of Management at the University of Arizona and holder of the Halle Chair in Leadership.

Richard Ravitch, Lieutenant Governor of the State of New York.

Harry Richardson, James Irvine Chair of Urban and Regional Planning in the School of Policy, Planning, and Development and Professor of Economics at the University of Southern California, Los Angeles.

Susan Rose-Ackerman, Henry R. Luce Professor of Jurisprudence (Law and Political Science) at Yale University and Codirector of the Law School's Center for Law, Economics, and Public Policy.

J. B. Ruhl, Matthews and Hawkins Professor of Property Law at Florida State University College of Law.

James N. Sanchirico, Associate Professor in the Department of Environmental Science and Policy at the University of California, Davis.

Ross Sandler, Professor and Director of the Center for New York City Law at New York Law School.

Joel Schwartz, Senior Consultant with Blue Sky Consulting Group.

Sam Schwartz, President and CEO of Sam Schwartz Engineering.

Philip Sharp, President of Resources for the Future.

Gerard Soffian, Assistant Commissioner for the Division of Traffic Management, New York City Department of Transportation.

Barton H. "Buzz" Thompson, Jr., Parry L. McCarty Director of the Woods Institute for the Environment at Stanford University, Robert E. Paradise

Professor of Natural Resources Law at Stanford Law School, and Senior Fellow at Stanford's Freeman Spogli Institute for International Studies.

Annie Weinstock, Senior Transportation Planner, Sam Schwartz Engineering.

Jonathan B. Wiener, Perkins Professor of Law and Professor at the Nicholas School of the Environment and at the Terry Sanford Institute of Public Policy at Duke University.

INTRODUCTION

A school of fish. Paige Gill/NOAA.

CHAPTER 1

Coping with Complexity
The Schooling Fish

The federal environmental statutes frustrate protection of the environment by requiring agencies to use methods that are unworkably centralized and complex. The Clean Air Act is one example among many. It commands the Environmental Protection Agency (EPA) to use exacting regulatory systems with the admirable goal of protecting us from each pollutant at each point in the country. The systems must take account of emissions caused by not only power generation and manufacturing, but also the design of vehicles, the driving habits of motorists, the layout of highways and mass transportation, the operation of every sort of building from hospitals to homes, excavation, farming, auto-body repair, dry cleaning, and many other activities. These systems limit emissions from many kinds of sources, including the industrial processes within particular factories. As a practical matter, specific limits often apply to different smokestacks within a factory, and factory managers frequently feel constrained to use the pollution-control technology that regulators had in mind in setting the limits.[1]

Other statutes follow this same hierarchical method. They require the EPA to adopt highly prescriptive controls to reduce water pollution, clean up old toxic-waste dumps, prevent further releases of toxic wastes, regulate pesticides, oversee the introduction into commerce of new chemicals, assure that tap water is safe, and more.[2] These systems, too, must achieve their objectives in all places and with regard to all relevant pollutants, hundreds of which science has identified.

This way of pursuing environmental goals far exceeds the EPA's capacity. In 1995 the two-time EPA administrator William Ruckelshaus wrote: "Any senior EPA official will tell you that the agency has the resources to do not much more than ten percent of the things Congress has charged it to do." The problem is that the job is so big, not that the resources are so scant. The EPA has substantial forces at its disposal. Its staff numbers almost twenty thousand, making it the largest federal regulatory agency.[3] In addition, Congress has endowed it with statutory powers to conscript a substantially larger number of state officials to enforce EPA requirements.

As a result, the EPA administrator sits atop a hierarchical chain of command that reaches down through various headquarter offices to regional offices, states and localities, and finally businesses and other targets of regulation. Detailed orders go down the chain of command, and detailed reports are required to come back up. This is a hierarchical system of control, par excellence.

The fundamental barrier to getting the job done is that Congress has charged the EPA with dealing with a complex environment through a method of regulation that is defeated by complexity. Even if Congress gave EPA a blank check to bulk up its staff, the chain of command would still end in a small group of leaders at the very top. No matter how brilliant, they would still have only so much brain power to process information and to devise detailed prescriptions in an effort to dictate to a complex and constantly changing mass of activities across a vast and diverse country.

We can pursue our environmental goals more effectively and efficiently by adopting less rigid and cumbersome methods. How to do so is suggested by the way schools of little fish scribe the contours of a coral reef and evade predators. Their environment is complex and dangerous. The reef has myriad contours, many with jagged edges; predators come in many forms and from many angles. Yet, these ever-changing threats evoke fast responses within the school. The fish in their hundreds or thousands respond quickly, seemingly as a single body, continually creating patterns of breathtaking beauty. Were a choreographer to chart the movements through which a corps de ballet might imitate the fish, the dancers would need weeks of rehearsal to turn the choreographer's prescriptions into a dance that replicates the school's ripples and shimmers. Yet, the fish, with no choreographer, no rehearsals, and small brains, coordinate effortlessly and respond almost immediately.

The fish are not dancing or aspiring to beauty; they are just trying to survive and flourish. But, to carry out group tactics to evade predators yet avoid collisions, they need to coordinate, and they can do so well and quickly because of, rather than in spite of, having no choreographer. What turns the fish into a school is individual fish responding to each other rather than to a leader.[4] As Professor Iain Couzin observes, "Individuals tend to maintain a personal space by avoiding those too close to themselves; group cohesion results from a longer-range attraction to others; and animals often align their direction of travel with that of nearby neighbours. . . . By adjusting their motion in response to that of near neighbours, individuals in groups both generate, and are influenced by, their social context—there is no centralized controller. . . . Close behavioural coupling among near neighbours . . . allows a localized change in direction to be amplified, creating a rapidly growing and propagating wave of turning across the group."[5] So, when some fish in a school evade an approaching predator, the whole school responds.[6]

The norm that determines how individual fish move relative to their neighbors means the fish work as a network. By network, we mean a group of entities—be they fish, humans, or computers—linked by a norm that allows them to coordinate.[7] So, for example, a standard protocol allows many computers to communicate and thus makes them into a network.

It is essential that the fish work as a network rather than as a hierarchy. A hierarchy can't be any smarter than the leaders on top, which is fine when the leaders are intelligent and the environment relatively simple, but not when it is complex. A network can, in contrast, be much smarter and more observant than any of its individual members because information is gathered and processed at many points.[8] Not only can a network of fish adapt faster than a brilliant choreographer can dictate to a corps de ballet, but a network of personal computers can outperform a mainframe, and a network of buyers and sellers—that is, a market economy—can generally allocate scarce resources more efficiently than a hierarchically directed economy, even if the chief of central planning is a genius. Similarly, a hierarchically controlled infantry can effectively focus great fire power in a simple context such as an open plain, but in the complicated context of a dense jungle it may lose out to more lightly armed commandos trained to function as a network.

A network is not, however, better than a hierarchy for every challenge. Infantry would blow away commandoes on an open plain. Moreover, as the recent economic crisis has reminded us, regulators have a vital role to play in enforcing norms necessary to keep a market network from breaking down.[9] In fact, we often combine network and hierarchical organization, the right combination changing with the challenge and the time. Hierarchical generals dictate the standards of operations for networks of commandoes and order them to achieve specified objectives.

In 1990, Congress successfully used a network to deal with a long-festering environmental problem, acid rain. The legislators felt pressure to cut the sulfur dioxide emissions from power plants that caused the problem but hesitated because a solely hierarchical approach would have effectively required the plants to install specific pollution-removal equipment at a price that would raise electricity rates sufficiently to anger voters. Legislators from the states where the plants were located wanted the cost to be shifted to electricity consumers in the downwind states that complained about acid rain. Legislators from those states disagreed. Cheaper ways were often available, but figuring out the right combination for each power plant —and the even more daunting challenge of finding a cost-efficient allocation of the cleanup burden among plants—was too complex and too fraught with distributional controversy for hierarchical regulation. By the end of the 1980s, this regional conflict had prevented the EPA and Congress from taking any meaningful action for more than a decade, despite mounting criticism.[10]

The breakthrough came in 1990, when Congress mandated an alternative to traditional hierarchical regulation that was supported by every living American Nobel Laureate in economics and some environmentalists. Instead of dictating how much sulfur dioxide each plant could emit or what equipment it should install, Congress created a straightforward standard of conduct: each power plant must have a government-issued allowance for each ton of emissions. Congress gave these allowances in proportion to a plant's past fossil fuel usage, permitted them to be bought and sold, and ensured that the total amount of allowances available would be capped, with the cap declining over time to ensure that overall emissions from power plants would be 50 percent lower than 1980 levels by 2010.[11] This approach is called "cap and trade" because the government caps the total amount of allowances and permits them to be traded. The declining cap forces reductions in total emissions. The trading of allowances means that the reductions can take place at the plants that can accomplish it most cheaply. Because allowances command a positive price in the trading market, firms face continuing incentives to find better and cheaper ways to reduce their emissions and make a profit by selling excess allowances.

Now, almost two decades after 1990, it is clear that cap and trade was a success. It vastly simplified the governmental job by outsourcing to the market the choice of who cuts pollution. Yet, cap and trade is far from laissez-faire. Just as a school of fish must skirt a jagged reef, so too must power plants in the aggregate bring total sulfur dioxide emissions down to the declining cap. But just as no one tells each fish just how to skirt the reef, no one tells each power plant how or where to reduce the pollutant. In both cases, a network decides how to adapt. What holds the pollution control network together is the standard Congress created: allowances whose possession permits a plant to emit a quantity of sulfur dioxide.

Congress was able to break the logjam on acid rain only because cap and trade promised to cut the cost of doing so and thereby eased the regional conflict between upwind and downwind states. Cap and trade is, in fact, delivering on its promise. By 2007, sulfur dioxide emissions had gone down 43 percent from 1990 levels, at costs substantially lower than under traditional command regulation. Electricity consumers, plant owners, and their stockholders saved many billions of dollars. The cost savings were possible because plant operators rather than EPA officials got to decide which sources would reduce emissions. This enabled plants to make the cuts at the places and by the methods that cost the least. In contrast, regulators lack the information to do so. Moreover, because allowances trade at substantial prices, the drive for profits would spur innovations to cut emissions. In contrast, hierarchical regulation provides neither flexibility nor incentives for green innovation. Yet, the entire cap-and-trade program is run by fewer than fifty people at EPA.[12]

Hierarchical vs. Network vs. Command-and-Control

The military term for close top-down control, "command-and-control," is sometimes used to characterize environmental regulation of the sort that we term "hierarchical." We avoid the term "command-and-control" because it has generated debates about whether those who use it have exaggerated the degree of centralized control. So we stick to the terms "hierarchical" and "network."[13]

The success of cap and trade on acid rain has helped produce a broad consensus in the United States for making it, or another network approach, such as a tax on greenhouse gas emissions, the centerpiece of any regulatory program to deal with climate change. Europe has already adopted a cap-and-trade approach despite initial skepticism. In the United States, the House of Representatives in 2009 passed a bill that includes a cap-and-trade program for regulating greenhouse gases, although it also contains strong hierarchical controls as well.[14] A market-based network approach is necessary for climate change because it is an especially complex and costly problem. Because of the diversity among us and the dynamic character of our economy and society, cutting greenhouse gases will require innovations not only in how electricity is generated but also in how transportation and much else is fueled, the design and operation of homes and workplaces, the distances between them, how agriculture and forestry are carried out and still more arrangements. The changes cannot come through the one-size-fits-all rules that hierarchical regulatory systems tend to use. Cap and trade and other economic incentive systems are powerful but efficient tools because they send a price signal to every consumer of energy that says "cut your contribution to greenhouse gases or pay."

The same logic that supports market-based network approaches for acid rain and climate change should lead to their application to other complex environmental problems. Federal statutes, however, still mandate the cumbersome hierarchical approaches that Congress adopted in the early 1970s, when modern environmental protection was in its infancy. Congress, of course, did not set out to lumber agencies with impossible jobs. In 1970, when it enacted what still remains the basic structure of the Clean Air Act, little thought had been given to cap and trade or other network approaches. Meanwhile, the hierarchical approach achieved some substantial progress at first. At the outset, regulators went after obvious ways to cut pollution, such as requiring large factories to install affordable tech-

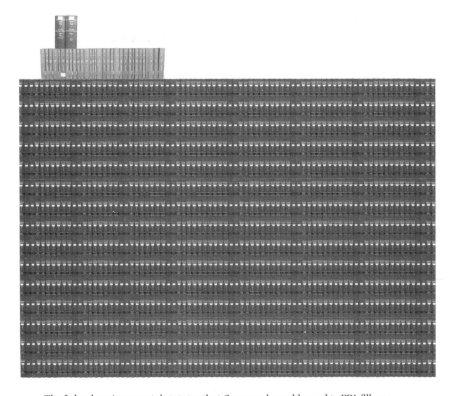

The federal environmental statutes that Congress has addressed to EPA fill more than 2,700 pages, represented by the two large United States Code volumes in the top row. The legally binding regulations issued by EPA to implement these statutes fill the 31 volumes of the Code of Federal Regulations in the next row. The guidance and other documents issued by EPA to explain or interpret its regulations fill around 1,000,000 pages, represented by the 1,250 loose-leaf volumes in the remaining rows. © 2009 Regina Chung, Director of Creative Services, New York Law School.

nology on smokestacks. Since then, however, the regulatory job has gotten much more complicated. With the low-hanging fruit having been picked, additional reductions require regulatory measures that are more far reaching, complex, and difficult. They require more expensive control technologies, altering the internal operation of industrial processes, and going after smaller sources. Moreover, the number of pollutants has grown from a handful to hundreds, and the number of pollution sources that need to be regulated to achieve environmental goals has mushroomed as well. Also, concern has broadened from pollutants released into the air and water to include those released into the ground and contained in products.[15]

The EPA has dealt with this growing complexity the only way it could—by bureaucratic means. The upper levels of the environmental chain of command lay on orders in copious detail, not only through regulations but through lengthy "guidance documents," as illustrated above.[16] These federal documents, however, represent only the tip of the regulatory iceberg. Additional layers below include state plans, statutes, regulations, and permits, all orchestrated by federal law. But not all decisions come from on high. Plant operators are allowed to make proposals and can litigate. State regulators and federal regional offices have a degree of discretion on some issues. The system is, however, essentially top-down.

This bureaucratic system tends to mandate uniform solutions when there are smarter ways to approach local conditions that would bring more environmental gain for less economic pain. So narrow is the focus on regulating even small emissions from a plant in highly specific terms that much larger emissions from the same plant are sometimes missed altogether. This hierarchical system also breeds litigation. Environmentalists frustrated by delay and lack of progress bring suits to force EPA to act faster. Industry, burdened by a plethora of complex and often dysfunctional controls, sue EPA to obtain some relief.

The hierarchy-heavy approach has come close to reaching its limits on some environmental problems.[17] It is widely understood that we cannot achieve our increasingly ambitious goals with the old statutes.

The Need for Fundamental Statutory Change

It hardly needs saying that no petty adjustment of the current set of laws can easily achieve . . . [environmental] objectives.
—William Ruckelshaus, 1995[18]

The problems [with the pollution control regulatory system] cannot be fixed by administrative remedies, pilot programs, or other efforts to tinker at the margins. They are problems that are built into the system of laws and institutions that Congress has erected for over thirty years. We recognize the difficulty of ever achieving fundamental, nonincremental change in the American government, but nothing short of such change will remedy the problems we have identified.
—J. Clarence Davies & Jan Mazurek, 1998[19]

Nearly 30 years ago Congress constructed a national framework of policies to protect the environment. It rested on a foundation of ideas that reflected the political and economic currents of that time. The structure has now been expanded and remodeled by 14 Congresses and six Presidents. Its existence is remarkable. But it is also ungainly and complex, and everyone agrees that it suffers from structural cracks. The foundation has shifted as times have changed and the building needs to be adapted to new underpinnings and new uses.
—Mary Graham, 1999[20]

The times are changing, and regulation should change with them. Regulation as we know it is due, not just for a tune-up but for a more basic overhaul that will make it more relevant and effective in a new era of environmental problem solving.
—Daniel J. Fiorino, 2006[21]

Future gains in environmental quality may be impossible without a fundamental reconsideration of regulatory design.
—Marc Allen Eisner, 2007[22]

Pollution, wastes, and chemical hazards are not the only environmental problems that hierarchical regulation has failed to solve. Take the depletion of ocean fish. Regulators responsible for some fisheries in federally controlled parts of the oceans announce that, once the total catch of a particular fish by commercial boats reaches a certain limit for the year, they will ban fishing for the rest of the year. In response, boats race to catch a lot in a hurry before the limit is reached. During the resulting derby, boats may fish around the clock and regardless of weather. When the Alaska crab fishery was regulated in this way, exhausted crews working in bad weather were killed and injured in such numbers that it inspired a television series, *The Deadliest Catch*. Meanwhile, with the entire year's catch reaching processors in a short period, the prices fishermen received plummeted. Speaking at the conference out of which this book grew, David Festa, an advocate from the Environmental Defense Fund, explained that this approach is "why virtually all of the fisheries around the world are being driven to over fished status."[23] The best hope, one that Festa favors and that is discussed in Chapter 6, is for regulators to empower a network of fishing-boat operators to decide how to stay within the annual cap by giving them tradable permits in a share of the catch.

At the same conference, a parallel account came from John Leshy, a veteran of the Natural Resources Defense Council and a law professor. Federal agencies allow ranchers to graze over a vast expanse of public lands, over a quarter billion acres, located mostly in western states. Despite their theoretically broad regulatory powers, federal agencies fail to stop the ranchers from grazing so many head of livestock that the land is stripped of vegetation, the soil eroded, and the streams muddied. The overgrazing has gone on for decades, including the eight years when Leshy served by appointment of President William Clinton as chief lawyer at the Department of the Interior. To reduce the overgrazing, Leshy favors introducing a new market element into the grazing permits that would allow conservationists to buy and retire them.[24] Chapter 6 will also discuss this and other property right-like approaches to conserving natural resources.

Network tools, although they come in many varieties, as the reader will see, should never fully supplant hierarchical regulation, or anything like it, but we need a much bigger dose of them in the mix because it is naive to suppose that the many failures of the hierarchical approach will be overcome simply by waiting for voters to elect a president with more environmental zeal. Such failures have persisted through presidential administrations of many different stripes. The president and Congress are subject to political pressure not just from factory owners but from farmers, consumers, employees, ranchers, and other voters, all of whom are affected by the wasteful costs and rigidities imposed by hierarchical regulation.

To make progress despite such pressures, we must have smarter governmental tools that pay dividends to both the environment and the economy. The reason being that voters want prosperity as well as environmental quality. That can happen only with the innovation spawned by network tools. This was the message to the "Breaking the Logjam" conference from Daniel Esty, director of the Yale Center for Environmental Law and Policy and former deputy chief of staff to the EPA administrator William Reilly: "[Government] has to be cleverer in how it structures incentives and regulations to . . . ensure that it's not a few thousand smart folks at the EPA thinking industry by industry about what pollution control technology to mandate as best available technology . . . but rather engaging millions of businesses, millions of smart people, millions of people who face regulatory burdens already and understand the environmental challenges of their own industries."[25]

Better regulatory tools must be the main driver toward green innovation. Such innovation is needed to tackle many unsolved environmental problems and must take many forms, not only high-technology inventions but also low-technology adaptations that can bring greener ways of doing things, starting with reducing greenhouse gas emissions. This is too much innovation to be purchased by the limited government fisc or mandated by rigid hierarchical regulation.[26] Better regulatory tools are the only affordable way to spur innovation and investment of the scope required.

The heavy reliance on hierarchical regulation not only frustrates green innovation but forces the federal government to conscript the states. So big is the job of issuing detailed instructions to many hundreds of thousands of regulated entities throughout the nation that the EPA cannot do the job alone. It must have help from the states. So many of the statutes mandate states to regulate or induce them to do so with federal grants.

Having the states implement federal statutes comes at a heavy price. The EPA loses direct control of sources of national and international importance and must, to boot, undertake the complicated and politically touchy job of supervising how states make and enforce rules. Moreover, the federal regulators end up supervising states on quite local environmental problems. This multiplies the EPA's duties, and the duties are usually enforceable in court.[27]

Tied down by a host of smaller localized problems with the minutiae of hierarchical regulation and often having to work through the states rather than directly, the EPA is distracted from solving the big problems that only the national government can fix. When scientists determine that an air pollutant is more dangerous than originally thought, it takes the EPA more than ten years, often a lot more, to cut public exposures through cumbersome federal-state processes. Congress sets deadlines for the agencies, but most of them are not met, regardless of the party in control of the White House.[28] Moreover, overwhelmed as it is, the agency is, as discussed, forced to bureaucratize, adopting detailed instructions that often leave insufficient room for states and localities to adapt to local variations and try innovative approaches. In sum, the old statutes' overreliance on hierarchical control leaves us with an allocation of responsibility that is the worst of both worlds: a federal government unable to deal expeditiously with national problems, and states and localities constrained by uniform federal dictates in designing solutions to local problems in light of local conditions.

Network tools, however, provide a way out of this trap of overwhelming complexity, inefficiency, delay, and litigation. By using them to simplify the regulatory job, the federal government could directly regulate those sources requiring national attention without having to go through the states. The federal job can be further and appropriately simplified by leaving some local problems to states and their subdivisions that have much more knowledge of local conditions, backed up, where needed, with federal safeguards. For example, Chapter 5 shows that federal cap-and-trade regulation of only three thousand sources of the most important pollutants could supersede the current system in which the federal government tries to make states regulate hundreds of thousands of sources of the same pollutants.

Network tools also avoid another malady of our obsolescent statutes: the statutes often ignore the trade-offs between environmental protection and other goals. The statutes enacted in the early 1970s generally told agencies to protect health without regard to cost or to reduce pollution as much as feasible without regard to the environmental benefit, as if countervailing considerations should be irrelevant. Whether they should be, they cannot be. For example, because most air pollutants pose health risks at any level, regulators must decide how much to reduce the risk and that requires considering whether a reduction in risk is worth the burden and cost. As a result, the regulators under every presidential administration have had to engage in trade-offs, but the statutes force them to pretend to the public that they don't. Network tools, in contrast, force the trade-offs into the open. With cap and trade for example, setting the cap means facing the trade-offs.[29]

Further network tools help with still another malady of our current statutes: the statutes too often ignore the crosscutting nature of environmental problems. So compartmentalized are their elaborate systems of detailed controls that, in solving one problem, they sometimes exacerbate other problems. For example, the EPA sets water pollution standards in terms of pollution concentrations in the discharge stream, which encourages sources to dilute their discharge with more water, which in turn works counter to the EPA's mission to conserve water. The hierarchical approach gives regulators such a complex job that they are driven to a high degree of compartmentalization. Network tools, in contrast, simplify the regulatory task and so make it easier to see the forest for the trees.

Accordingly, we propose that Congress and the president follow these principles to reform the environmental statutes:

Principle 1: Traditional hierarchical regulation should be complemented by new tools that deploy market- and property right-like mechanisms, such as cap-and-trade programs and information disclosure, whenever they can reliably achieve environmental objectives.

Implementing this principle would help advance three additional principles that would make government more effective, more open, and less blinkered in protecting the environment:

Principle 2: Authority should be realigned so that the federal government has direct responsibility for national and transnational environmental problems, and states and their subdivisions have more independent responsibility for essentially local ones.

Principle 3: Trade-offs should be faced openly and made on the basis of reliable information.

Principle 4: Regulatory approaches should be crosscutting and address underlying causes.

These four principles are not new. Environmental scholars from the left and right have advocated them, but often one at a time and generally in abstract terms.[30] Our "Breaking the Logjam" project differs by proposing concrete reforms based upon all four principles on a comprehensive range of environmental challenges with a continued effort to push these proposals to help ensure that they are implemented. We are sticking to the question of how government should structure itself to clean the environment—which, after all, is the subject of all four principles—and stay away from the question of "how clean is clean enough?" Nonetheless, that very question will be highly relevant in legislative consideration of our proposals to restructure environmental protection. Environmental advocates will oppose the legislative bills that implement the principles if the bills' environmental objectives are weak and would lead to backsliding in environmental quality. Similarly, businesses will oppose bills that implement the principles if the bills would increase compliance costs too dramatically. The point is that tools capable of coping with complexity such as those used to break the logjam on acid rain provide ways to improve the environment at moderated cost. The principles can pay environmental and economic dividends so that there is plenty of room for a win-win step forward.[31]

CHAPTER 2

How We Got Lost in Complexity
The Mistaken Squirrel

A squirrel crossing a country road stops in the middle, notices your oncoming car, and takes a few hops back the way it came. You slow down to give the creature time to get off the road, but it reverses direction again, and then again, remaining in your path. You slam on the brakes, but too late to stop. You hope it eluded the wheels and mutter about its infuriating indecisiveness.

Gray squirrel (*Sciurus carolinensis*). © 2003 Calvin J. Hamilton.

Actually, the squirrel has decisively implemented a tactic evolved to meet a threat from a predator such as a fox. "When [the eastern gray squirrel] is caught unawares in the open by a predator at some distance . . . this species shows the typical single erratic display of so many mammals, swerving, zigzagging, and stopping at irregular intervals until it reaches a tree or other object up which it can climb. . . . [This behavior] becomes much more pronounced in frequency and irregularity of turns when the animal is approached closely by a predator."[1] Unfortunately for the squirrel, the threat comes from a four-wheeled vehicle rather than a one-mouthed fox. An erratic move may take the squirrel away from one wheel but under another. In mistaking a driver who wants to avoid it for a predator who wants to eat it, the squirrel has used obsolete tactics.

Like the squirrel facing the modern car, the United States facing the modern environmental threat is stuck with obsolete tactics. Our statutes are obsolete in four ways:

1. Overreliance on hierarchical regulation.
2. Misalignment of power between the federal government and the states.
3. Hiding of trade-offs between environmental protection and other goals.
4. Compartmentalization of crosscutting problems.

Our statutes have these characteristics because their basic structure dates from a time, the early 1970s, when we conceived of modern environmental problems as if they were a singular, short-term threat such as a fire or flood threatening to engulf a city. When they burst upon the scene, the environmental perils seemed stark—air so polluted that children had to be kept home from school, a river so polluted that it burned (or so it was reported), and offshore oil leasing so haphazard that a well hemorrhaged petroleum for ten days.[2] The threat was all the more dire from the federal perspective because the distrust of the southern states on civil rights carried over into a distrust of states generally on the environment.

The response of Congress to environmental threats in the early 1970s parallels in some ways how threatened communities once dealt with emergencies such as a potentially all-consuming fire or flood—by putting themselves in the hands of a commander empowered to order whatever it took to eliminate the threat. Similarly, the modern environmental statutes put society under the direction of federal agencies (hierarchical regulation, federal conscription of states and localities), spared no effort to stem the perceived emergency (ignoring the trade-offs between environmental protection and other concerns), and dealt in this way with each new crisis separately as it hit the headlines (compartmentalization of cross-cutting problems). The statutes promised to eliminate each emergency in short order—to put out the fire. For example, the 1970 Clean Air Act came with the promise that "all Americans in all parts of the country shall have clean air to breathe within the 1970's." Similarly, the 1972 Clean Water Act set out to make all waters in the United States "fishable and swimmable" by 1983 and to eliminate "the discharge of pollutants into the navigable waters" by 1985.[3]

To deliver on these promises, the statutes created a series of duties designed to ensure success. For example, the 1970 Clean Air Act provided (and still provides) that, to establish mandatory national clean air goals, the EPA must promulgate National Ambient Air Quality Standards. To achieve those goals in every region, states must implement plans that impose controls on emission sources; and to fulfill these state implementation plans, pollution sources must carry out the controls. As the Supreme Court put it, Congress "had taken a stick to the states." The statute set deadlines for each of these duties, the final deadlines came due before the end of the 1970s, and each duty was enforceable by citizen suit. This lockstep strategy, which persists today with revised and postponed deadlines, was designed to eliminate any slack that could jeopardize fulfilling the statutory promises.[4]

These statutes received overwhelming support from Democrats and Republicans in both the House and Senate. In enacting the statutes, the leaders in Congress and the president focused more on comforting voters and not letting political opponents get all the credit than on how the statutes would work in the long run. That was anybody's guess, because never before had the United States undertaken a sustained peacetime program to mobilize such economy-wide efforts to achieve such utopian goals through detailed regulation. The statutory schemes were simple enough in concept—define the environmental goal, develop plans and regulations, implement and enforce—but applying the scheme to a complex society could not be simple.[5]

The tools in the environmental statutes were adopted on the theory that they would curb the emergency in a relatively few years. Yet, unlike a fire or flood threatening a city centuries ago, which would have triggered temporary emergency powers to deal with a temporary crisis, the modern environmental problems persist. The tools in the modern environmental statutes, though suitable to an emergency soon to be contained, are no good for the long run. Hierarchical regulation, when overused, brings sharply diminishing returns, crimps society more than necessary to stop antisocial conduct, and thus spurs resistance and undercuts its own moral legitimacy. The upshot is that the scheme is never fully implemented.[6] Like the squirrels, we have adopted tactics poorly suited to a threat like the one we face today.

We are, of course, smarter than squirrels, so we should be more capable of correcting mismatches between old tactics and new threats. Indeed, we have discerned the mismatches. In the United States, scholars, advocates, and government officials of the left, center, and right have documented them for many years. Yet, the statutes remain remarkably the same in strategy and structure as they were in the 1970s. There has been no major federal environmental legislation since the Clean Air Act Amendments of 1990; in fact there has been a marked slowing down of any environmental legislation since then (see table 1).[7]

With Congress logjammed, agencies are left to "portage" around the faults in the statutes as best they can. For example, the Department of Interior under President William Clinton made the rigid terms of the Endangered Species Act somewhat more flexible and functional through imaginative administrative practices. However, political vulnerability and legal challenges limit the power of regulators to work around legislative paralysis through administrative portages. The statutes are so long and detailed that many administrative fixes are vulnerable to legal challenge, and it takes only one environmental advocate or business to bring a lawsuit that could stymie years of administrative effort. For example, the EPA under President Clinton in 1998 and then under President Bush in 2005 extended to other air pollution problems the cap-and-trade approach that Congress had in 1990 applied only to acid rain. The agency was careful to limit these rules to subsets of pollution problems. Even so, a court of appeals found that the 2005 extension violated the statute. The decision upset not only regulators but also industry and environmentalists, who thought cap and trade a better approach than traditional hierarchical regulation. The court nonetheless felt duty bound to uphold the dead hand of past Congresses as reflected in its reading of the statute.[8] So agencies tend to be cautious in their portages.

Why, despite the evolving understanding of the environmental challenge, are we stuck with environmental statutes whose structure dates back to the era of the phonograph record? One reason is that the Constitution was designed to make it difficult to enact statutes. The House, the Senate, and the president are all involved, and it is hard to secure agreement on basic changes. The Constitution created these hurdles to prevent ill-considered statutes, but they also make it more difficult to update obsolete ones.

Yet this difficulty can be overcome—and has been on occasion. Both parties in Congress and the administration of George H. W. Bush cooperated in enacting the 1990 air pollution legislation that

Table 1. Notable Environmental Legislation, 1970–Present

1970s	1980s	1990s	2000s
National Environmental Policy Act of 1969 (1970)	Alaska National Interest Lands Conservation Act (1980)	Clean Air Act (1990) Oil Pollution Act (1990)	
Clean Air Act (1970)	Comprehensive Environmental Response, Compensation, and Liability Act (1980)	Safe Drinking Water Act (1996)	
Federal Water Pollution Control Act (1972)		Food Quality Protection Act (1996)	
Federal Insecticide, Fungicide, and Rodenticide Act (1972)	Resource Conservation and Recovery Act (1984)		
Noise Control Act (1972)	Comprehensive Environmental Response, Compensation, and Liability Act (1986)		
Coastal Zone Management Act (1972)			
Endangered Species Act (1973)	Safe Drinking Water Act (1986)		
Safe Drinking Water Act (1974)	Toxic Substances Control Act (1986)		
Forest Rangeland Renewable Resources Planning Act (1974)	Emergency Planning and Community Right to Know Act (1986)		
Federal Coal Leasing Act (1976)	Safe Drinking Water and Toxic Enforcement Act (1986)		
Toxic Substances Control Act (1976)	Clean Water Act (1987)		
Resource Conservation and Recovery Act (1976)	Federal Insecticide, Fungicide, and Rodenticide Act (1988)		
National Forest Management Act (1976)			
Federal Land Policy Management Act (1976)			
Clean Air Act (1977)			
Clean Water Act (1977)			
Surface Mining Control and Reclamation Act (1977)			
Outer Continental Shelf Lands Act (1978)			

brought the cap-and-trade approach to acid rain, but not to other air pollution problems. Unfortunately, the working relationship between Congress and that administration fell apart not long thereafter. The first president Bush ran for the White House vowing to be the "environmental president" and appointed the president of the World Wildlife Fund, William F. Reilly, as his EPA administrator. However, this president's hopes to re-create bipartisanship on the environment were disappointed. "No matter what he did," writes Professor Richard Lazarus, "the environmental community seemed only to criticize his administration for not doing enough." Thus rebuffed, Bush later brought his policies more in line with the wishes of those who would support him: the business community.[9]

Since then, the bipartisanship necessary for retooling the environmental statutes has vanished. There might have been an opportunity under William Clinton. He was no environmental firebrand as governor of Arkansas, and while president he had worked with Republicans to reform welfare. His "Reinventing Government" agenda suggested openness to network approaches and realignment of responsibilities between federal and state governments, something that actually was accomplished in welfare.[10] The opportunity to cross the partisan divide on the environment was, however, wasted. The leader of the Republicans in the House of Representatives, Newt Gingrich, won control of Congress for his party in the 1994 congressional elections under the banner of his

---

Note for Table 1
NOTE: Table 1 is based on Richard J. Lazarus, *The Making of Environmental Law* (Chicago: University of Chicago Press, 2004), 70, 107, 110–12, 125, and Jonathan Weiner, "Radiative Forcing: Climate Policy to Break the Logjam in Environmental Law," 17 *New York University Environmental Law Journal* 210, 211 n.3 (2008). This table is the product of these authors' judgments as to what legislation is "environmental" and what environmental legislation is worth noting. Although there is room to differ on such judgments, changing the characterization of a few of them would not change the overall picture of Congress's having done relatively little in recent decades to revise its handiwork in light of experience. The statutes are listed by shortened name; some are amendments of previously enacted statutes with the same name.

"Contract with America." But he overplayed his hand on environmental regulation, seeking rollback more than reform. As Professor Lazarus observes, "If even a pretense of nonpartisanship was then possible, the Democratic members of Congress and the Clinton administration eliminated it altogether by their response. Democrats seized the political initiative, either because they legitimately believed that Republicans sought to eliminate meaningful environmental protection or because they perceived a political opportunity to weaken the political opposition. In either case, the resulting rhetoric furthered the partisan divide."[11]

The environment had become a wedge issue in an era of wedge politics. Both parties played to their bases: environmental advocates lined up with Democrats and business lined up with Republicans. The divide grew even wider under President George W. Bush. The issue of the environment turned into the "Hatfields and Mc-Coys" in Congress, according to E. Donald Elliott, an observer respected by both camps. "Both sides," he remarked, "preferred an 'issue' that they could use with their constituency to portray the other side as unreasonable rather than a compromise."[12] No wonder there has been a logjam on environmental legislation since 1990, or that the basic structure laid down in the 1970s has not evolved despite three decades of experience demonstrating the need for change.

The partisanship that poisons environmental reform in Congress also affects agencies, reinforcing caution about administrative innovation by heightening political vulnerability. Elliott observed that "the politicization of environmental issues has gotten so bad that when a Republican Administration *tightens* air pollution rules set by its predecessors it is roundly criticized for *weakening* them, on the grounds that it could have tightened them more, a feat of language that would make George Orwell proud."[13]

Ironically, some of the federal statutes' obsolete features contribute to the legislative logjam. Take the failure to face trade-offs in the statutory mandate that the EPA protect health without regard to cost. When business interests sought legislation requiring that the EPA forgo pollution reduction measures whose cost was disproportionate to the health benefits, environmentalists charged that business wanted to sacrifice human health because of corporate greed. The result was a stylized debate in which both parties played to their base, thereby contributing to the paralyzing polarization.[14] In private, however, all sides recognize that, although pollution often poses real risk of serious harm, trade-offs at some point well short of zero risk are necessary and appropriate, although of course there are substantial disagreements about how to make them. Yet, it's hard to introduce such nuance into a legislative mandate to issue hierarchical regulations to protect health without regard to cost, because either cost counts or it does not, like a light switch that is either on or off. In contrast to hierarchical regulation, network approaches shift the focus from such a question of high principle to concrete questions of degree. For example, in setting a cap for cap and trade, one group of legislators might want to cut a pollutant by 60 percent, and another by 35 percent. At this concrete level, an intermediate number offers a ready compromise.

As another example of how the statutes' obsolete features contribute to the legislative logjam, consider that the statutes call for the EPA to conscript the states to carry out a nationally designed approach not only to nationally important issues but also to highly localized ones. As a result, any legislation to modify the national design affects a multiplicity of localized issues. Congress is understandably asked to look at the consequences of proposed legislation, but it lacks the bandwidth to reconsider such a broad array of politically touchy issues. So, instead of fixing the wholesale problems in the statutes, its environmental committees tinker at retail to address limited problems, through oversight hearings and the paraphernalia of the appropriations process, such as riders, earmarks, and directives in committee reports. In this way, members of Congress continue to seek credit for being active on the environment without having passed any important authorizing statutes since 1990. Many years ago William Ruckelshaus, once again, said what needs to be said: "Congress is going to have to return to its constitutional role of setting national policy and providing vigorous oversight, and leave EPA to get on with implementing that policy, free of direct supervision from 535 administrators."[15]

These two features of the statutes that discourage reform—the pretense that there need be no trade-offs and the conscription of the states—have their root cause in another and more pervasive obsolete feature of the statutes, overreliance on hierarchical regulation. As discussed in Chapter 1, that overreliance has led Congress to conscript the states to do work that the federal government should do directly, to hide trade-offs, and to compartmentalize interconnected issues. If Congress could bring itself to update the mix of legal tools in the statutes to include an array of network solutions (thus vindicating our first principle of reform), it would well be on its way to addressing these problems (thus vindicating the other three principles as well).

Fundamental change requires leadership. But we have a Congress and a president who ran promising to reach across partisan divides. They were elected by voters who in 2008 selected presidential candidates for both major parties, each vowing action on climate-change, embracing cap and trade, and in general playing to the middle on environmental issues.[16]

Congress, for its part, is confronted not only with intense demand for action on climate change and other problems but also with equally intense concern about the economic impact of such action. The competition between concern for environmental quality and concern for economic prosperity that underlies the logjam presents politicians with the toughest sort of political problem, the distributional problem of how to "divide the pie." Successful politicians sometimes solve such distributional problems by finding ways to enlarge the pie. That was what Congress did in 1990, when it adopted the cap-and-trade approach to acid rain. Because it produced more environmental progress at significantly less cost, every side got more than would have been available if acid rain had been addressed under the old hierarchical approach. This book suggests similar win-win solutions to many current environmental issues through new combinations of tools that would allow making sense of federal-state arrangements, prompt facing trade-offs in the open, and reduce the compartmentalization of environmental issues. Other publications of the project apply this approach to more problems.[17]

To match the environmental protection system to present-day problems, Congress must undertake wholesale change in the statutes, starting with the mix of regulatory tools. Retail tinkering will leave us, like the squirrel, continuing to hop back and forth in the middle of the road.

REFORM

Beavers in their environment. Picture Collection, The New York Public Library,
Astor, Lenox and Tilden Foundations.

CHAPTER 3

Principles of Reform
The Adapting Beaver

By building and maintaining a dam, beavers transform a stream into a pond in which they build their lodge and stockpile their food. Once they consume their favorite food species in the vicinity of the pond, they move on, and the old dam, no longer maintained, is swept away. Eventually, the food species regrow, and the beavers return. After many repetitions of this cycle, so much sediment from the still waters behind the dam settles in the pond that it can turn into a lush meadow, much different ecologically from the woods and stream that had been there. The beaver has rightly been called an "ecological engineer." Its engineering has also help set the stage for changes in its own genes through natural selection. Having long constructed watery worlds, the beavers now have not only their trademark flat tails and webbed rear feet, the better to swim, but also valves in the ears and nose that close during dives and built-in swimming goggles in the form of transparent eyelids.[1]

Humans, like the beaver, change the earth, and like the beaver's, the changes we have wrought in the earth have altered how we function, though in our case through our legal institutions. This legal evolution is a constant process of change, feedback, and adaptation. Early civilizations adopted laws to protect the environment from destructive human activity, as they understood it.[2] New understandings, new technologies, and new lessons about the successes and failures of the old laws brought new environmental laws over many centuries. So much was new on all these fronts in the mid-twentieth-century United States that it produced the remarkable environmental statutes of the early 1970s.

Since then, both the environmental problems and our understanding of them have continued to evolve. Experience with the hierarchical tools mandated in the statutes of the early 1970s not only brought progress but showed their inherent limits. There was little, if any, thought of employing network tools when Congress set the basic structure of modern environmental law in the early 1970s. Where the new tools have been tried, they have produced important gains, partly because large businesses have become more environmentally aware and adaptive over the past few decades. Almost all major corporations recognize that they must operate in a political climate that precludes open disdain for environmental objectives. So they have hired large environmental health and safety staffs with the training to take constructive advantage of flexibility, where it is offered.[3]

Environmental groups are different too. Many that previously relied almost exclusively on litigation have economists on their staffs and hire investment bankers and consultants to appeal to corporations on the basis that environmental responsibility is good business.[4]

Individuals have changed as well. The *New York Times* reports on "what experts say is a growing army of 'eco-kids'—steeped in environmentalism at school, in houses of worship, through scouting and even popular culture—who try to hold their parents accountable at home." Some consumers buy their solar panels and Priuses, even when it does not pay. For a tiny savings on their groceries, they bring in their own bags not just to upmarket Whole Foods but to mass market Price Chopper.[5] Market-based regulatory and information programs will generate incentives and information to strengthen and broaden such behavior.

None of this suggests that government should stop using its coercive power, but it does suggest that using that power increasingly through network tools, including cap and trade, has more potential today than it would have had in the 1970s.

Similarly, states and localities have changed. In the late 1960s, some states had risen to the environmental challenge faster than the federal government, but by the 1970s the ambition of the federal government's programs was well in front of almost all states. Since then, however, the federal government has too often fallen short of most of its promised goals. States were in front in controlling especially hazardous air pollutants in the 1980s and then on climate change and oceans early in the twenty-first century.[6]

Moreover, disparities between states in support of environmental protection are currently less pronounced than they were. Income differences between regions have evened out. News coverage has broadened understanding of environmental concerns. It is no wonder that public support for environmental protection is increasingly widespread. In the early 1970s, elites led the demand for environmental protection, whereas advocates for racial minorities and the poor saw the environmental issue as a diversion. Today, the demand for environmental protection is wider. Membership in the many national environment groups has risen spectacularly (for example, the count for the Natural Resources Defense Council went from the low thousands in the early 1970s to over a million in the early twenty-first century). In addition, there are thousands of state and local environmental groups.[7] Minority communities are now deeply concerned with environmental quality and have organized accordingly.

In sum, the hierarchical approach in the old statutes has helped produce conditions that set the stage for new approaches. Yet, despite the ecological succession in our understanding of the environmental challenge, the basic structure of environmental law institutions remains stuck in the 1970s. This refusal to act on the lessons of experience should, and must, eventually come to an end.

As William Ruckelshaus wrote in 1995 (to reprise the opening epigraph of this book), "At some time in the future—probably when this current version of gridlock is more apparent—we will be able to deal seriously with the reform we all recognize is needed. What would that reform look like?"[8] That is the question to which we now turn. This chapter examines four principles drawn from experience to guide statutory change. Later chapters turn these principles into concrete recommendations in specific fields.

Principle 1: Traditional hierarchical regulation should be complemented by new tools that deploy market and property right-like mechanisms, such as cap-and-trade programs and information disclosure, whenever they can reliably achieve environmental objectives.

Here we amplify the brief description of cap and trade provided in Chapter 1 and go on to review other new tools that many scholars have advocated.[9]

With cap and trade, government communicates differently than with hierarchical regulation. With hierarchical regulation, government talks to each individual plant in terms of quantities ("your plant cannot emit more than so much") or on occasion specified techniques ("your plant will have to install this pollution control equipment"). With cap and trade, government talks to individual plants in terms of price ("your plant will bear a cost for emitting pollution"). The reason is that each unit of pollution that the plant emits means having to buy one more allowance or selling one less.[10]

What makes cap and trade a network approach is that government sets a standard (in the case of acid rain, emit no more than you hold allowances for) that prompts separate firms or individuals to cooperate to reach government's objective (in the case of acid rain, staying within the cap).[11] The network gets to the goal more efficiently than could hierarchical regulation because it is in the interest of plants for which emission cuts are relatively inexpensive to make them and sell allowances to plants for which emission cuts are more expensive. Hierarchical regulation, in contrast, must generally impose uniform requirements on all plants in a category because there are hundreds or thousands of them, and regulators lack the administrative resources and access to information needed to determine which plant can do what most inexpensively and to tailor individual plant requirements.

Besides, to the extent that hierarchical regulation seeks to assign more of the cleanup burden to plants that can do it most economically, it ends up giving an advantage to the others that use inherently dirty techniques. That's unfair, and it's bad for the environment and the economy. In contrast, cap and trade rewards firms that use inherently cleaner production techniques.

Indeed, the cost of allowances gives plant managers a powerful reason to find and use innovative ways to reduce emissions more effectively and economically. With hierarchical regulation, plant managers have no such incentive because emissions up to the mandated emission limit are free. To the contrary, hierarchical regulation gives plant managers an incentive *not* to develop innovative ways to reduce emissions. The reason is that regulators are supposed to require plants to reduce pollution as much as feasible, so that the consequence for a company of finding a better way to reduce pollution is bearing the expense to install it.[12]

Because cap and trade produces more pollution reduction for less cost, it enables society to achieve more ambitious environmental goals with less burden on society, as the acid rain program demonstrates.[13] It can pay off on established problems for which hierarchical regulation has had initial success, such as air and water pollution from large facilities, but is having trouble eking out further progress at tolerable cost (see Chapter 5). It can also pay off handsomely on many new problems, such as climate change, because price signals provide a way to stimulate the vast array of high-tech and low-tech adaptations needed to make progress (Chapter 4). It can also help with natural resource problems, such as depletion of fish stocks (Chapter 6). It is less intrusive and rigid than hierarchical regulation and can therefore make gains without drawing so heavily on the scarce political and moral capital of environmental regulation.

To attain environmental goals reliably, however, cap and trade must punish deviations from the standard that emissions not exceed allowances held. The acid rain program mandates automatic penalties for violations; compliance has been outstanding, higher than with ordinary hierarchical regulation.[14]

Strict enforcement in turn requires monitoring the sources of emissions. With cap and trade, regulators can no longer check compliance by finding whether a source uses a certain control method, but instead must gauge its emissions. They can do so under the current cap-and-trade program for sulfur dioxide emissions from power plants because the statute resulted in most plants installing equipment that continuously monitors emissions. Affordable monitors are not, however, presently available for some other categories of pollutants and sources. The EPA should develop workable monitoring methods for additional categories, as the National Research Council has recommended. For many categories for which direct monitoring is not yet feasible, emissions can still be reliably estimated, and developing methods to do so should also be a priority for the EPA. Meanwhile, cap and trade should be applied only where regulators can determine how much each source emits with a degree of reliability commensurate with the environmental stakes.[15]

Because cap and trade does not control *where* pollution is emitted, but only the total amount, government must also be alert to the possibility that trading might concentrate a dangerous amount of emissions in a particular locale. Such hot spots do not arise with greenhouse gases, because they mix globally; where they are emitted is irrelevant to their environmental impact. That is not necessarily true of most air or water pollutants, however. Nonetheless, air pollution hot spots are, according to a National Research Council report, possible in theory but unlikely in practice, at least for the widespread pollutants subject to National Ambient Air Quality Standards, and have not occurred in previous cap-and-trade programs. At the same time, *not* adopting cap and trade carries risks of hot spots because total emissions will be higher with no guarantee that they will be spread evenly. Proposals to substitute cap and trade for hierarchical regulation must consider the risk of hot spots and include safeguards when needed, as the National Research Council recommends.[16]

Cap and trade is only one of several market-based alternatives to hierarchical regulation. Another is called "credit-offset." This system imposes a baseline regulatory limit on every source (for example, no more than a set amount of emissions per ton of steel produced or of lead per gallon of gasoline refined) but lets sources that do better than the limit get credit that can be sold to other sources, which can use it to offset emissions exceeding their baseline regulatory limit.[17]

Still another market-based mechanism is a tax or a fee on pollution or other activity that harms the environment. The tax or fee, like cap and trade and its cousin, credit-offset, sends a price signal to reduce environmental harm and provides the flexibility to decide how to do so. In the United States, environmental fees are used to encourage the return of beverage containers, lead-acid batteries, and other products. Environmental taxes and pricing are used in a number of European countries to achieve a variety of goals, including the reduction of carbon emissions, air and water pollution, and traffic congestion in cities. The success that London and other world cities have had with congestion pricing has led several cities in the United States to consider following their lead.[18]

Network approaches other than market-based mechanisms include creating property-like rights in natural resources to augment regulatory schemes to protect natural resources. For example, John Leshy and Molly McUsic suggest supplementing the current, largely unsuccessful regulatory scheme to prevent ranchers from grazing too much livestock on public lands by granting these

ranchers and conservation groups a right they do not now have—
to sell and buy the right to retire the land from grazing. (See Chapter 6.)

Another network approach is the disclosure of information on
environmental impacts. In 1986, for example, Congress required
companies to report their release of toxic chemicals. This information was made available on the Internet, searchable by zip code.
The disclosure resulted in a marked decrease in toxic releases.
Firms reacted out of fear that reports of high releases would expose
them to private litigation, precipitate adverse decisions by state and
local governments, and hurt their standing with consumers, investors, and the general public. Also, the monitoring and reporting
required by the law alerted businesses that the releases constituted
a loss of commercially valuable product and that they could often
save money by capturing the chemicals and reusing them rather
than releasing them into the environment.[19]

This mandate to provide information on the release of toxic
chemicals is a network approach, because government sets a common standard for disclosing information and thereby facilitates
cooperation among a wide variety of actors. Informational approaches, unlike market-based approaches, do not attach a price to
pollution and other environmentally harmful activity directly, but
they nonetheless create incentives because the information influ-
ences consumers, investors, voters, employees, and other actors. In
most cases, information disclosure alone will not be enough, but it
can fill gaps left by regulation and provide the information that leads
to smarter regulation. The impact of informational approaches can
be heightened by prodding firms to consider and address environmental impacts as part of their internal business management practices. Environmental regulators encourage such practices by taking
a tougher approach on enforcement against firms that lack them.[20]

There are many other government mandates to disclose environmentally important information. California requires that
businesses warn people before exposing them to toxins in products.

The Securities and Exchange Commission requires firms to disclose potential environmental liabilities.[21]

Even without government mandates, environmental organizations and private firms have established eco-labeling regimes—for example, on whether sustainable methods are used in producing wood or catching fish. Government can add credibility to these efforts by setting labeling standards, especially on such vague terms as "organic."[22]

Congress should also direct the federal government to provide the public with more pointed information about the environmental performance of governments at the state and local levels. Governors and mayors do not want their jurisdiction to be near the top of the list of pollution levels any more than they want to be high on the list of crime rates, especially when states and localities try to attract jobs by advertising the quality of their environments.

What should not be lost in the multiplicity of network tools is that we have learned a lot since the late 1960s and early 1970s, when markets were thought to be the cause of environmental problems, and hierarchical regulation the solution. Today, it is widely agreed in policy circles that network approaches, including those that are market-based, are often good tools to solve many pollution and natural resource problems when properly designed and implemented (see box on page 42). Strong bipartisan support for such market-based mechanisms is evident in the major bills introduced in Congress to deal with climate change.[23] We need to expand our use of these market-based mechanisms to address not only climate change but other environmental problems, both old and new. Of course, the right choice of network tools and the balance between them and hierarchical regulation will vary with the context.

Network Tools

Market incentives should be used to achieve environmental goals, whenever appropriate.
    —President Bill Clinton and Vice President Al Gore, 1995[24]

Market mechanisms can work. In fact, they have worked exceptionally well in a number of areas across the United States. Of course, economic instruments, as they are sometimes called, are not panaceas. . . . Policymakers at all levels of government, in partnership with private businesses and nongovernmental organizations, should reinvigorate their efforts to develop and implement a next generation of economic incentives.
    —Robert Stavins and Bradley Whitehead, 1997[25]

Congress should . . . authorize EPA and the states to implement allowance-trading systems to reduce pollution in air and water, explicitly liberating such systems from the constraints of traditional facility-based permitting, provided that trades would not result in unacceptable risks in local areas.
    —National Academy of Public Administration, 2000[26]

While I am a strong supporter of expanding the use of environmental markets, trading and other incentive-based systems, and also of information creation and disclosure programs, I recognize that even these are *not* the Holy Grail of environmental institutions. There are no perfect institutions.
    —E. Donald Elliott, 2001[27]

Cap-and-trade programs have been shown to be effective at achieving emission reductions at much less cost to the regulated facilities than traditional technology-based or performance-oriented standards.
    —Committee on Air Quality Management in the United States, National Research Council, 2004[28]

Wherever possible, policies should be reconfigured to minimize the reliance on command-and-control instruments and maximize the reliance on cap-and-trade instruments that have a proven track record of attaining higher levels of environmental quality at lower costs.
    —Marc Allen Eisner, 2007[29]

A cap and trade system . . . is a smarter way of . . . controlling pollution than dictating every single rule that a company has to abide by, which creates a lot of bureaucracy and red tape and oftentimes is less efficient.
    —Barack Obama, 2008[30]

Principle 2: Authority should be realigned so that the federal government has direct responsibility for national and transnational environmental problems, and states and their subdivisions have more independent responsibility for essentially local ones.

One justification sometimes offered for federal regulation is that all Americans should have a right to a healthy environment and that the federal government is the natural protector of this right because its authority spans the country. Many people are attracted to the concept of such a right, or at least to certain basic environmental protections. But regardless of whether individuals should have such a right and what its precise content might be, the language of rights is not helpful in determining how to allocate responsibility for environmental issues between the states and the federal government. Determining what level of government should take responsibility for environmental issues ultimately requires making pragmatic choices on an issue-by-issue basis.

Pragmatism calls for division of labor. The aim should be for the federal government to have and use the tools to solve national problems without having to work through the states, and for the states to solve local problems without having to answer to the federal government, subject to federal backstops to safeguard national concerns.

The landmark federal environmental statutes of the 1970s did not provide for a sensible and effective division of labor. As a necessary consequence of relying on hierarchical regulation, the statutes conscripted the states to implement federal regulatory requirements. Thus, federal agencies had to work through the states to solve national problems. Moreover, because the statutes also made the federal agencies ultimately responsible for solving most environmental problems, the states had to answer to federal regulators, even on highly localized matters. Some good has come of this strategy. Federal mandates increased the environmental competence of state governments and improved environmental quality.[31] Now, however, that state governments are more competent, public concern for environmental quality is more widespread, and exclusive reliance on hierarchical regulation is no longer a given, it is time to reconsider the allocation of power and responsibility set by the 1970s statutes.

Experience has shown that the existing allocation has often proved excessively rigid and complex and has fallen short in environmental protection. When the federal government has to work through the states, the response to environmental problems is slowed. For example, when the EPA decides that a pollutant subject to a National Ambient Air Quality Standard is more dangerous than previously thought, it cannot simply tell sources to cut emissions; rather it must embark upon a decade-long process in which it revises the standard, tells states how to develop state implementation plans to achieve it, awaits state plans, and reviews them, all as a prelude to emissions actually being cut.[32]

Moreover, when states and localities must do things the federal way, as dictated by remote federal bureaucracies, it is difficult for citizens to understand and participate in the resolution of environmental issues that are close to home. At the same time, because federal agencies are responsible for almost every environmental problem, no matter how local, they are overburdened. This leads them to adopt cookie-cutter standards that ignore local variations. It also means they drain their capacity to deal with problems that require resolution at the national and international level.

States, in recent years, have in significant respects been more aggressive than the federal government in protecting the environment. While environmental protection in Washington has been gridlocked for decades, states have moved forward. When the federal government preempts state regulation that is stronger than federal regulation—as it often has been recently—we are denied the benefits of worthwhile state and local efforts to protect health and the environment, from which we can all learn.[33]

Yet, many environmental problems require direct federal regulation, notwithstanding the problems of centralization. For example, the federal government should step in when activities within a state do harm elsewhere. States whose plants release emissions that spill over into other states may underregulate their polluters because the victims of the pollution are out-of-state residents who do not vote in the polluting states. Similarly, federal control of endangered species and treasured national parks and forests, although located in a single state, is justified because Americans living in other states have a substantial stake in their preservation. Federal regulation may also be warranted when separate state regulation of goods would hobble trade or prevent economies of scale in manufacturing.

Moreover, the case for national control is particularly strong when it is necessary to work with other countries and international organizations to address environmental issues that are international or regional in scope. Problems such as climate change, protection of marine ecosystems and resources, and preservation of biodiversity cannot adequately be addressed by any country acting on its own.

Today, many policy analysts from across the political spectrum believe that the time is overdue for a fundamental reassessment that would take due account of the character of different environmental problems and the appropriate contributions that different levels of government can make in solving them (see box on page 46).

Realigning Responsibility between Governments

We have certainly learned that Washington, D.C., is not the source of all the answers. There is growing support for sharing decision-making by shifting more authority—and responsibility—from the Federal government to states, tribes and local communities.
    —President Bill Clinton and Vice President Al Gore, 1995[34]

EPA and Congress need to hand more responsibility and decision-making authority over to the states and localities. EPA still needs to set and enforce national standards for environmental quality and pollution control in order to prevent states or cities from victimizing their neighbors. However, a new partnership needs to be formed, one based on "accountable devolution" of national programs and on a reduction in EPA oversight when it is not needed.
    —National Academy of Public Administration, 1995[35]

[We need] a more rational allocation of decisionmaking authority in the environmental arena between the federal government and the states.
    —Richard L. Revesz, 1996[36]

Recognizing that there is an important role for government in protecting the environment does not answer the question of what level of government should act. . . . [The concerns of some recent environmental reformers] about overly rigid policies dictated from Washington that do not match local needs and circumstances often strike a responsive chord. . . . But decentralization is not always the right policy answer. A more refined line of analysis suggests that environmental policies should match the scale of the problems to which they are addressed.
    —Daniel C. Esty and Marian R. Chertow, 1997[37]

I favor an increased degree of decentralization as a way of making environmental protection more effective, not as a way of undermining it.
    —Daniel A. Farber, 1999[38]

The issue of how to divide federal and state authority is not a question of how national policy can prevent a "race to the bottom" among states in order to minimize environmental protection. The language of the 1970s does not describe federal-state relations 30 years later and does not help policymakers approach the next generation of environmental problems. . . . The tough questions are not whether federal or state authority should rule, but how to combine their force effectively.
    —Mary Graham, 1999[39]

The role of EPA in establishing and implementing national and multistate emission-control measures should be expanded so that states can focus their efforts on local emission concerns.
    —Committee on Air Quality Management in the United States, National Research Council, 2004[40]

Congress should allocate responsibility to federal, state, and local governments according to their comparative advantage in dealing with various environmental issues. The federal government's environmental workload should be geared to what it can intelligently and effectively manage. When Congress adopts legislation to address climate change, implementing this new regulatory regime will be the top priority of the federal environmental bureaucracy. The Environmental Protection Agency and other federal agencies need to be given the space to focus their resources on this new challenge and on other environmental issues that cross state or national lines. In some cases this will require expansion of existing federal authority, while in others, especially with regard to local environmental problems, it will require a greater state role.

The principle of matching regulatory responsibilities to the most suitable jurisdictional scales is straightforward enough in the abstract, but it is less clear how it should be applied to specific environmental issues. There are issues on which the underlying considerations pull in different directions. For example, greenhouse gases emitted in one state cause harm nationally and globally and therefore call for control at the national and international level. But, to the extent that their control requires changes in building codes to reduce energy consumption, it is difficult to imagine the federal government taking over the job of building codes from state and local government. In the end, our proposals seek to reconcile such competing concerns on an issue-by-issue basis.

Even when states should have primary responsibility, the federal government can often play an important supportive role. For instance, it often will be cheaper for the federal government to fund and synthesize scientific research about environmental problems that occur in many states, thereby saving state governments the cost of replicating that research.[41] The federal government already provides information on pollution levels, trends, health and welfare effects, and control techniques to the states and the public, and could do so on an even broader scale. Such federally provided information arms citizens with an understanding of environmental threats and their sources and thereby generates pressures on state and local officials to do well relative to other jurisdictions. In sum, federally provided information is a way to help state and local government do a better job.

Principle 3: Trade-offs should be faced openly and made on the basis of reliable information.

When the Clean Air Act passed in 1970, the dividing line between unhealthy and clean seemed as obvious as the plume from a filthy industrial smokestack. Against this background, the statute called for the EPA to set National Ambient Air Quality Standards to protect health and welfare, without regard to the costs of abating air pollution, and gave every citizen a legally enforceable right to the attainment of those standards. Yet, the language of rights has proved to be more confusing than helpful. Today we know that there is no clear dividing line between safe and unsafe air quality. As previously noted, trade-offs between risk and cost are inevitable. That is even clearer now that pollution levels are generally much lower, instruments are available to detect pollutants at levels near zero, and the techniques exist to predict risks at levels so low that the control costs to eliminate them altogether approach infinity.

In principle, there is no problem with Congress placing a much higher value on the benefits of clean air than on the costs. But the statute tells the EPA not to sully environmental protection by weighing benefits against costs at all, even though that is impossible. In reality, regulators have silently ignored this rhetorically attractive but utterly impractical direction. The EPA under every president has considered regulatory costs and burdens, as well as the benefits in setting these standards.[42] So the EPA engages in trade-offs. Although the statute forces it to deny that it does so, EPA also makes covert trade-offs by not pressing deadlines and by tolerating noncompliance by states and industry when the costs and disruption of enforcing absolutist mandates are too great.

Other statutes similarly prevent open discussion of trade-offs. The Endangered Species Act, passed in 1973, requires all endangered species to be listed without regard to the cost of protecting them and mandates that agencies automatically protect all listed species. Yet, the agencies cannot adequately protect most of them because Congress does not provide the necessary resources.[43] Congress trumpets that it embraces absolutist environmental standards and then undercuts those standards through a practically invisible bureaucratic process where the trade-offs get made.

In some cases, the unrealistic absolutism of the statutes drives the agency into paralysis. For instance, the EPA accomplished very little from 1970 through 1990 under the Clean Air Act provision calling for regulatory elimination of all risk from especially hazardous air pollutants; it gave so little scope for prioritizing that the agency refused to undertake any regulation at all of most of these pollutants.[44]

In general, many statutes fail to provide mechanisms for making trade-offs in the open. Into this vacuum, presidential administrations have inserted an administrative system requiring agencies to conduct cost-benefit analyses of new regulations and alternatives, subject to review by the Office of Management and Budget (OMB), even where the statute mandates that cost not be considered in the final decision. Having long been used by administrations of both parties, this practice is now entrenched, though sometimes criticized for anti-regulatory bias.[45] Despite its importance, Congress has never addressed its application in most statutes. Indeed, because many statutory provisions fail to acknowledge the possibility of trade-offs, cost-benefit analysis usually never appears on the legislative or judicial radar screen.

Many policy analysts from across the political spectrum argue that the time has come to face the trade-offs openly and on the basis of reliable information (see box below). Going forward, Congress should admit that trade-offs are inevitable and make them itself or speak to who should make them and by what method. The method should put the trade-offs in full public view and bring to bear reliable information. To the extent cost-benefit analysis is used, it must compare costs and benefits even-handedly.

The inevitability of trade-offs:

Environmental and other kinds of laws are cheapened if we continue to pretend that such considerations as costs are not germane to standard-setting, when in fact we all know they are. In other words, if we know about and implicitly accept such tradeoffs, why not sanction them in the law so that regulatory officials are forced to make tradeoffs in the open, where we can object if lives or amenities are taken too lightly in rulemaking.
　　—Paul R. Portney, 1990[46]

Tunnel vision, a classic administrative disease, arises when an agency so organizes and subdivides its tasks that each employee's individual conscientious performance effectively carries single-minded pursuit of a single goal too far, to the point where it brings about more harm than good. In the regulation of health risks, a more appropriate label is "the last 10 percent," or "going the last mile." . . . A former EPA administrator put the problem succinctly when he noted that about 95 percent of the toxic material could be removed from waste sites in a few months, but years are spent trying to remove the last bit. Removing that last bit can involved limited technological choice, high cost, devotion of considerable agency resources, large legal fees, and endless argument.
　　—Stephen Breyer, 1993[47]

The language produced by Congress, the pressures produced by the public, and the past promises produced by EPA have often converged on the question, "How can we make this situation 'safe?' This is a seriously deceptive formulation and hence a wrong question. Often safety is simply impossible. . . . The question EPA should ask is, How much should be spent to achieve how much health risk reduction for different segments of the public—in light of both the costs and the uncertain consequences of such efforts?
　　—Marc K. Landy, Marc J. Roberts and Stephen R. Thomas, 1994[48]

In addition to the mistaken belief that absolute safety is both possible and affordable, the theory was that if standards were set extremely high, sometimes on scant scientific evidence, and an extremely tight time frame was set to achieve those standards, then there would be constant pressure on industry and on EPA to make continuous improvements. The nation was committed to a sort of pie-in-the-sky at some future date, a

date extended further and further as inevitably EPA missed nearly every deadline set for it. Each time a new generation of clean technology came into use, the response from EPA had to be. "That's great—now do some more," whether that "more" made any sense or not.
      —William D. Ruckelshaus, 1995[49]

Congress often deceives the public by conveying the notion that environmental regulations can provide absolute safety: scientific findings indicate that for many, perhaps most, pollutants safety is a matter of degree and absolute safety is unobtainable. Both Congress and the executive branch shrink from conveying to the public the difficult trade-offs that environmental decisions often entail, and the public encourages such deception by wanting absolute safety at no economic cost in the same way it wants more government services and lower taxes. A better-educated public would reduce the temptation of government officials to practice such deception.
      —J. Clarence Davies and Jan Mazurek, 1998[50]

Systematic approaches to making trade-offs:

EPA should refine and expand its use of risk analysis and cost-benefit analysis in making decisions.
      —National Academy of Public Administration, 1995[51]

While economic analysis should not replace political judgment in a democracy, it should inform the decision-making process and help encourage more effective and less wasteful regulation. Assessing the strengths and weaknesses of regulatory proposals can ensure a consistent, systematic measurement of the relevant benefits and costs across agencies.
      —Robert W. Hahn and Robert E. Litan, 1997[52]

Cost-benefit analysis often helps to identify the best tools for achieving social goals. A significantly reformed system of regulation could save many lives and also many billions of dollars.

The chief advantage of cost-benefit analysis is that it can get the effects of various approaches on the table, helping to spur government action where the problem is genuinely large and helping to dampen intrusive regulation where there is little reason for concern. . . . If people choose to proceed even though the costs outweigh the benefits, they are certainly entitled to do that, certainly if they can identify some reason for proceeding. At least cost-benefit analysis will help show them what they are doing.
      —Cass R. Sunstein, 2002[53]

Cost-benefit analysis not only . . . is inevitable, but also . . . it is desirable. We live in a world of finite resources. Some social problems will resist being resolved, even if we spend every dollar we have to address them.
      —Richard L. Revesz and Michael A. Livermore, 2008[54]

Following our first two principles would help lead Congress in this direction. Cap and trade, for example, requires setting a cap that overtly addresses how far to go to achieve environmental objectives. The realigning of national and state responsibility so that each takes direct responsibility for the problems would also help to expose trade-offs and promote accountability for their resolution. By announcing an absolutist environmental goal and mandating that the states achieve it, Congress has sundered the political and other benefits and burdens of achieving the goal. Congress gets to claim credit for protecting the environment, and states are forced to deal with the costs. When the federal government takes charge of delivering on its promises through systems of direct regulation such as cap and trade, however, both the benefits and costs fall on the same level of government and so make the trade-offs and the responsibility for making them more apparent. The same results follow when state and local governments are in charge of local problems.

Principle 4: Regulatory approaches should be crosscutting and address underlying causes.

The governmental structure adopted in the statutes of the 1970s compartmentalizes environmental protection. Many of these statutes assign responsibility to the Environmental Protection Agency, but despite its sweeping title, it shares responsibility for environmental protection with many other federal agencies. These include the Fish and Wildlife Service and the Bureau of Land Management in the Interior Department; the Forest Service in the Agriculture Department; the National Oceanic and Atmospheric Administration in the Commerce Department; and the Army Corps of Engineers in the Department of Defense. Even the EPA is divided into distinct offices that operate largely independently of each other, such as those for air pollution and water pollution.[55]

The compartmentalization is dysfunctional because with environmental protection, as with the natural environment itself, everything is connected to everything else. Piecemeal steps to decrease air pollution have increased water pollution, steps to decrease water pollution have increased disposal of toxics on land, and cleanup of toxics on land has led to air or water pollution.[56] Compartmentalization and bureaucratic tunnel vision produce regulatory measures that reduce a targeted environmental risk but produce others as a byproduct.

As it is now widely recognized (see box on page 54), a more holistic approach, or at least one more attuned to cross-over effects, would facilitate smarter environmental protection. For example, Chapter 4 urges that climate change should not be seen solely as a matter of the emission of greenhouse gases, such as carbon dioxide. Also included in the mix should be changes in forestry and agricultural practices that would increase the amount of carbon dioxide taken out of the atmosphere and put into plants. Chapter 6 points out opportunities for a more unified approach to oceans and ecosystem services. Nonetheless, some division of labor is inevitable. Chapter 7 points out ways to minimize its ill effects.

Crosscutting Strategies

Rather than focusing on pollutant-by-pollutant approaches, attention must shift to integrated strategies for whole facilities, whole economic sectors, and whole communities.
 —President Bill Clinton and Vice President Al Gore, 1995[57]

Whether the "patient" is an individual human or an ecosystem, those charged with reducing risk have subspecialized their roles into such finely targeted elements of the nation's risk portfolio that they have great difficulty anticipating and resolving the countervailing consequences of their efforts to reduce risk. Resolving risk tradeoffs would be more viable if decision-making institutions adopted a "whole patient' outlook for selecting the policies within their authority, and if some innovations in organizational structure were adopted to better link subspecialists to one another.
 —John D. Graham and Jonathan Baert Wiener, 1995[58]

The environmental control effort should be integrated. In consultation with Congress, and as part of the process of integrating the environmental statutes, the [Environmental Protection Agency] . . . should begin work on a reorganization plan that would break down the internal walls between the agency's major "media" program offices for air, water, waste, and toxic substances.
 —National Academy of Public Administration, 1995[59]

The fragmentation of the current [pollution control regulatory] system is a major factor in its lack of rational priorities, its inefficiency, and its difficulty in identifying and dealing with new problems. Within the next decade, most developed nations will have abandoned the medium-oriented system in favor of an integrated approach. The United States should not be saddled with an antiquated and cumbersome approach.
 —J. Clarence Davies and Jan Mazurek, 1998[60]

Over the years, federal and state governments have addressed environmental problems one at a time, constructing individual regulatory frameworks to deal with air, water, and land pollution. The cumulative result has been a proliferation of environmental baronies, located in various agencies, departments and congressional and state legislature committees.
 —Mary Graham, 1999[61]

The division of environmental laws, programs, and agencies along medium-specific lines tends to fragment regulatory strategies, leading to missed opportunities and higher-than-necessary compliance costs.
 —Daniel J. Fiorino, 2006[62]

The first two principles can help government deal with the crosscutting nature of environmental problems. The market-based approaches of the first principle can let distinct regulatory programs work together. As an example, if we deal with both climate change and traditional air pollutants subject to National Ambient Air Quality Standards (called "criteria pollutants") through properly linked cap-and-trade programs instead of hierarchical regulation, the programs will reinforce each other rather than clash, as will be shown in Chapters 4 and 5. More generally, market-based approaches simplify government's job, which makes it easier to see the overall picture and address linkages among parts. The old tools exacerbate compartmentalization because compartmentalization is the only way that the command structure can deal with the complexity. The new tools reduce regulatory complexity by outsourcing subsidiary decisions to firms and individuals through market and informational incentives.

Reducing regulatory complexity and compartmentalization is also achieved by the second principle of realigning the responsibilities of the federal government and the states. Instead of one level of government, the federal, overseeing the solution to all problems, states and localities would take charge of many problems. At these lower levels of government, it would be easier to see interconnections and relate different programs in their concrete application.

Not all environmental experts fully agree with the need to embrace fundamentally new regulatory strategies. These individuals are concerned with the unknowns in following new strategies and prefer to stick with the machinery they are familiar with, despite its limitations. The disagreements are, however, not along the lines of left-right, Democratic-Republican, or green-business. The principles set forth in this book find broad support from both sides of these divides. In the following chapters, we discuss concerns raised by skeptics about the application of these principles.

Turning the principles into concrete proposals requires judgment, because the principles are in tension at points and their application is sometimes a matter of degree. How to apply our four principles is accordingly somewhat indeterminate at the margins, but the principles do show which direction to go.

Although applying these principles will provoke disagreement and does require judgment, apply them we must. Otherwise, we will remain stuck with an environmental protection system ill suited to today's challenge. The challenge has evolved over the past forty years, as has our understanding. The environmental protection system should evolve like the beaver along with the challenge.

CHAPTER 4

Climate Change
The Combustible Rock

To moderate climate change requires cutting emissions of greenhouse gases (chiefly carbon dioxide, methane, and nitrous oxide), which keep energy from escaping from the earth's surface into space.[1] The leading culprit is the carbon dioxide that comes from burning oil, coal, and natural gas. It is easy enough for government to vow to cut carbon dioxide emissions but hard to determine precisely how to do so, at least without losing popular support. The problem is that burning such fossil fuels is basic to our economy. To burn less requires either constricting our economy (e.g., fewer goods and services), making the economy more energy efficient (e.g., more fuel-efficient cars, factories, and homes), or switching to energy sources that do not emit carbon (e.g., wind, solar, or nuclear). The range of possibilities is vast and ranges from the low-tech (retrofitting old doors and windows with weather stripping) to the high-tech (removing and sequestering carbon from power-plant smokestacks).

In deciding how to proceed, government might adopt a market-based approach, such as cap and trade or a tax, that would send price signals to cut greenhouse gas emissions. In that case, firms, households, and other energy users would individually choose where and how to cut. Alternatively, government could make those choices for us or at least narrow the options available. It could do so directly by issuing regulations or indirectly by subsidizing the development or use of select ways to reduce emissions. In doing so, government would substitute public choices for private ones.

Experience suggests that we should be cautious about government's ability to choose among competing energy technologies without bungling the job. Consider "oil shale," a sedimentary rock that contains neither oil nor shale, but does, like oil, contain ancient organic matter and is combustible. It has been used for fuel since prehistoric times. Although oil shale contains much less energy per pound than oil or coal, that energy can be extracted and concentrated into synthetic fuel. The earth contains so much oil shale that more fuel could be made from it than from all the world's petroleum reserves. According to a RAND Corporation study, "The largest known oil shale deposits in the world are in the Green River Formation, which covers portions of Colorado, Utah, and Wyoming." The study estimates the recoverable oil in this one area at 800 billion barrels, more than "triple the proven oil reserves of Saudi Arabia."[2]

United States government officials had hoped as early as World War I to use domestic oil shale to end dependence on imported oil. In 1949, the Department of Commerce predicted that oil shale could be converted into gasoline at 11.5 cents a gallon, less than its wholesale price. The federal government showed intermittent interest in developing the conversion process, and that interest grew after the Organization of the Petroleum Exporting Countries (OPEC) sharply cut oil exports, thereby causing traumatic price increases and shortages, first in the early 1970s and then again in 1979. After the second oil shock, President Jimmy Carter persuaded Congress to establish the Synthetic Fuels (Synfuels) Corporation, a federal enterprise that was supposed to be given $88 billion to develop oil shale and other synthetic alternatives to petroleum. Its first major expenditure was the Colony Oil Shale project in Colorado, sponsored by Exxon and Tosco; it floundered because of massive cost overruns.[3]

Despite funding many projects, the Synfuels Corporation yielded next to nothing for energy independence. While the rapid rise in petroleum prices had spurred public support for synfuels development, prices plunged soon after the corporation got under way. Carter's successor as president, Ronald Reagan, believed that government investment in synfuels businesses violated free-market principles. At his urging, Congress terminated the Synfuels Corporation in 1986.[4]

It would be unwise, however, to assume that a repeat attempt by government to pick energy technologies would produce better results. Rapid price fluctuations in petroleum and changes in administration policy have continued down to the present. Moreover, the whole Synfuels enterprise was plagued by serious problems of technology, cost, and performance. Under President Reagan, the Synfuels Corporation did back another big oil shale demonstration, the Parachute Creek project, sponsored by Occidental Petroleum and Tenneco. It even shielded the project from falling petroleum prices by guaranteeing to purchase its product at $60 to $67 per barrel when conventional petroleum was selling at $29. This plant experienced technological problems and delays, however, and was eventually abandoned.[5]

In retrospect, it is fortunate that the Synfuels Corporation failed in developing the technology of the Colony and Parachute Creek projects as an answer to our energy needs. It would have wrought environmental havoc. The technology required mining the oil shale, bringing it to the surface, heating it to extract the energy, and then disposing of the filthy spent shale. Doing this on a scale sufficient to produce much fuel would scar the land, consume scarce water, and pollute the air and water on a massive scale. Moreover, making fuel from shale consumes so much energy that switching from petroleum to shale-based fuel would increase greenhouse gas emissions.[6]

Government was no smarter at picking winning technologies when, much more recently, it backed corn-based ethanol, initially on the theory that it would improve air quality and later on the theory that it would help with climate change. It turns out that corn-based ethanol can in some circumstances do more harm than good on both air quality and climate change. It can turn wildlife habitat into corn fields, raise food prices, and enrich farmers at the expense of motorists. Government requires ethanol be added to gasoline and subsidizes ethanol producers; nonetheless, many of them still cannot turn a profit.[7]

Private firms, left to their own devices, also make mistakes in picking technologies. But there are many such firms, and the ones that get it right capture the market and reap the rewards. Where private firms often fall short is in neglecting aspects of the public interest, such as controlling pollution and reducing dependence on unstable energy sources, that do not translate into profits for firms. The beauty of network regulatory solutions such as cap and trade or taxes is that such solutions can marry the strengths of the government and the market by giving private firms a profit-based incentive to pick and adopt winning technologies that further the public interest. They can be used to deal with climate change without government trying to pick technological winners in the face of the inevitable distortions introduced by campaign contributions, voting blocs, and bureaucratic limitations.

The current Clean Air Act would require government to make public choices about which sources should cut greenhouse gas emissions and by how much. The Supreme Court has in essence ruled that the EPA must treat greenhouse gases as pollutants under the federal emissions-control provisions of the Clean Air Act. But that statute's provisions were adopted without climate change in mind. Indeed, some provisions of the Clean Air Act would be positively unworkable if applied to greenhouse gases. Doing so would increase by a hundredfold the number of sources requiring special federal permits and controls for major new or "modified" sources (New Source Review) and would include not only large factories but also many office and educational buildings, hospitals, and farms.[8] More generally, applying to greenhouse gases such source-specific requirements as New Source Review controls would restrict the flexibility that cap and trade or a tax would allow to achieve greenhouse gas emission reductions in an efficient way. Setting National Ambient Air Quality Standards for greenhouse gases makes little sense for multiple reasons, one of which is that concentrations are a product of emissions on an international scale. The response to climate change must, of course, include significant emission reductions by our nation, but market-based regulatory tools should be at the heart of our way to achieve them.

The EPA has yet to issue binding regulations under the Clean Air Act, and so there is no overhang of existing hierarchical regulations as of yet. For now Congress has a blank slate on which to prescribe a network regulatory approach. By seizing this opportunity, Congress can avoid the mistake of having government picking among technologies. In adopting market-based tools to regulate greenhouse gases, Congress should, in general, exempt them from hierarchical regulation under the existing Clean Air Act. The bill that the House of Representatives passed in 2009 provides for a broad exemption and does include a market-based approach, cap and trade. However, the cap will not require significant reductions in greenhouse gas emissions from fossil fuel combustion until 2025 or beyond. Until then, the bill's main impact on such emissions will come from hierarchical controls. They take three forms. First, sources get free allowances on the condition that they comply with requirements to use government-selected technologies to reduce emissions. Second, many other provisions of the bill mandate outright regulation. Third, still other provisions provide subsidies for government-chosen technologies. So, while the bill embraces a network approach in principle, it imposes many mandates and constraints on how private actors should go about reducing emissions and picks certain favored technologies.[9]

The leading market-based method of reducing greenhouse gas emissions is cap and trade. (Another possibility is taxing greenhouse gas emissions, to be discussed later.) A cap lets government decide how much to limit greenhouse gas emissions, but the trading feature outsources the decisions about where and how to stay within the cap. The gains from making these decisions through the market rather than hierarchical regulation will be even greater in the case of climate change than of acid rain because the variety of techniques available to reach the objective is much greater and the variations in the control costs among the many different activities generating greenhouses gases are much greater still.[10]

Whatever the size of the cap, it should decline over time. Firms argue that they should get the allowances for free, though giving them away would grossly overcompensate many firms.[11] On the other hand, auctioning all the allowances could likely bankrupt some firms, and there may not be enough liquidity in the economy for firms to buy enough allowances to create a smoothly functioning market. Whatever the merits of these arguments, any giveaway of allowances should be limited to a transitional period, after which all the allowances should be distributed by auction, if for no other reason than to keep climate objectives clear of a political scrum for immensely valuable assets.

Cap and trade can achieve the greatest reductions in greenhouse gas emissions at lowest cost if the cap applies to the widest possible range of activities and so brings into the program all the opportunities to cut emissions. That way, the market can sift through them all and achieve cuts at least expense. Thus Congress should impose a greenhouse gas cap that is economy-wide. In particular, the cap should include not only power plants and other large industrial sources but all uses of fossil fuels. For ease of administration, the cap should, to the extent feasible, be applied to the upstream suppliers of these fuels, such as petroleum refiners and coal companies, rather than to their ultimate consumers. The suppliers would have to make sure that they do not sell more carbon and other greenhouse gas precursors than they have allowances for. Although they would have to pay for the allowances, most of the cost would be passed down the supply chain to the ultimate users of the fuel, including motorists and users of heating oil. They would then get a price signal to reduce their use of fuel and thereby reduce their contribution to greenhouse gas emissions.[12]

This price signal would go not only to big businesses but to everyone else, including individuals and small businesses. "Everyone else," cumulatively, can achieve a major reduction in emissions, often at little cost. So long as government distributes the revenues from auctioning the allowances directly to us, or indirectly via tax cuts and credits, we are on average better off if the pressure to cut greenhouse gas emissions falls on everyone. If the burden is limited to emissions from big business, consumers end up paying through higher prices, and the total cost to us will be greater because broader opportunities for cheaper reductions have been missed.[13]

The cap-and-trade program should, in principle, apply to all greenhouse gases, not just carbon dioxide, as often proposed. However, the monitoring and administrative capacity necessary to keep track of emissions of some of these other gases may not yet be available. Instead of waiting until the capacity exists to keep track of all greenhouse gases, the cap-and-trade program should apply to carbon dioxide and the greenhouse gases that can be tracked and then be applied to other gases as the capacity to track them becomes available. In the interim, the cap-and-trade system should grant credit offsets for reducing emissions of any gases not initially covered. To ensure the integrity of the system, the program should establish conservative default methods for estimating reductions in these greenhouse gases.[14] Such a system would provide incentives to reduce these other gases and develop improved monitoring and verification methods. This credit-offset system would, however, fail to impose costs on those who continue to emit these other gases. For that reason, Congress should launch a program to equip government with the means to include more gases in the cap-and-trade program.

Additionally, the cap-and-trade program should, in principle, apply to every sector of the economy. However, the monitoring and administrative capacity necessary to keep track of nonfuel emissions of some sectors, especially agriculture, is not available yet. This problem requires a parallel response. Until such emissions can be put under the cap, the cap-and-trade program should grant to farmers, forest owners, and others credits for capturing extra carbon in forests, other vegetation, and soils.

While this cap-and-trade program should be federal, states should also be allowed to impose their own restrictions on sources of greenhouse gases. States have led the way on climate change. They should not be stopped from continuing to provide an impetus so long as their activities are not inconsistent with federal efforts. Congress should not preempt states from imposing tougher controls on federally regulated stationary sources.[15]

An alternative to cap and trade is a tax on greenhouse gas emissions. Both approaches send a price signal to reduce emissions. A tax does so by setting the tax rate. Cap and trade does so by reducing the quantity of greenhouse gas allowed to be emitted, thereby making the right scarce and therefore valuable. The tax sets the price signal directly, which indirectly reduces the quantity; cap and trade sets the total quantity directly, which indirectly generates a price signal. Both a tax and cap and trade would give complete latitude on where and how to reduce emissions and make it profitable to do so in the most economical ways, while encouraging the development of yet more economical solutions. The coverage of any tax program should parallel that of the cap-and-trade program discussed above.[16]

Much has been written on the comparative merits of the cap-and-trade and tax approaches and on intermediate approaches that blend their characteristics.[17] If a cap-and-trade program allows sources to buy additional allowances from the government at a "safety valve" price, it is effectively a tax to the extent that this safety valve is used. Also, if a cap-and-trade program involves auctioning of allowances, it resembles a tax in producing revenues. There are, however, critical differences between a cap and a tax. The cap focuses public attention on the amount of greenhouse gas reduction and promises certainty on it, but leaves the cost of the reduction more uncertain. In contrast, the tax focuses public attention on the cost of greenhouse gas reduction and provides certainty on it, but leaves the amount of the reduction more uncertain. Straddling these differences would be a cap with a safety valve or a tax with automatic increases if emission targets are not met.

The imperative need for an effective global regime to limit greenhouse gases makes cap and trade the better choice for the domestic program to reduce greenhouse gas emissions. Cap and trade is superior to the tax approach for an international agreement because it provides a readier way of accommodating the equity claims of developing countries and providing incentives for them to reduce their emissions. Because of their lower level of development and the greater responsibility of developed countries for existing concentrations of greenhouse gases, developing countries would never agree to a tax as high as that of developed countries without some sort of compensation. If the taxes are lower in these countries, industry would relocate to them, and so, to a considerable extent, the emissions would be moved rather than reduced. Inducing these countries to levy taxes as high as those in developed countries would require direct financial transfers from developed countries. This would entail government-to-government agreements on how much specified governments pay other governments and ongoing legislative appropriations in the various developed countries.[18] It would be much easier to meet the equity claims of developing countries through an international cap-and-trade system by giving them more generous allowance allocations. This would meet their concerns about undue limits on their development and create incentives for them to reduce emissions in order to sell surplus allowances to developed country firms. Once governments agreed on the allocations, the market could handle the intercountry transfers efficiently and create business opportunities for developed country firms selling and investing in climate-friendly technologies for developing countries. Finally, the European Union has a cap-and-trade system, and it is highly likely that any post-Kyoto international climate regime would also be based on trading rather than taxes. Although it would be theoretically possible for the United States to adopt a domestic tax program and still participate in an international cap-and-trade system, there would be many difficulties in meshing the two systems.

Whether Congress adopts cap and trade or a tax, changes in knowledge or circumstances may call for changes in the greenhouse gas program. The statute should call upon the EPA or another expert body to propose to Congress at set intervals (perhaps every five to six years) any needed changes.

Although a cap-and-trade or a tax program would send price signals that influence ways to reduce greenhouse gases emissions, some choices are not fully susceptible to price signals. For example, even with a vigorous cap-and-trade program, private firms would underinvest in basic research on techniques to reduce emissions where it is hard to patent all the beneficial applications, as is often the case. Government therefore does need to go beyond sending price signals, though they should remain the focus. As the economist William Nordhaus wrote:

> Whether someone is serious about tackling the global-warming problem can be readily gauged by listening to what he or she says about the carbon price. Suppose you hear a public figure who speaks eloquently of the perils of global warming and proposes that the nation should move urgently to slow climate change. Suppose that person proposes regulating the fuel efficiency of cars, or requiring high-efficiency lightbulbs, or subsidizing ethanol, or providing research support for solar power—but nowhere does the proposal raise the price of carbon. You should

conclude that the proposal is not really serious and does not recognize the central economic message about how to slow climate change. To a first approximation, raising the price of carbon is a necessary and sufficient step for tackling global warming. The rest is at best rhetoric and may actually be harmful in inducing economic inefficiencies.[19]

For this reason, government should limit its interventions to problems that cannot be cured by price signals. In particular, government should fund basic research and development in technologies that promote energy efficiency, renewable energy, and methods to capture and sequester carbon dioxide emissions.

On the other hand, subsidizing the use of renewable energy sources, either from the proceeds of allowance auctions or climate taxes or out of general revenues, is not a good long-term solution because the subsidies encourage energy use and could, if done to excess, substantially increase the overall cost to the public. Here again, it is pertinent that government is not good at picking the best technologies.[20] Subsidies may, however, play a constructive role in the short term. They can help start the move away from fossil fuels during the period before price signals from market-based regulatory approaches have fully kicked in and help produce economies of scale in production of energy from renewable sources. At this early stage, subsidies may also be needed for low income people who lack the capital needed to take measures such as insulating their homes to reduce energy use. A related but different problem is that a cap or a tax will fall more heavily on lower income people, but the preferable response is transfer payments or tax reductions rather than subsidizing particular technologies. In any event, subsidies for alternative energy sources and conservation are politically inevitable as a means of stimulating the economy in these challenging times. The point we emphasize is that such subsidies should be confined to this short-term role.

In the early stages of subsidies, their size should, to the maximum feasible extent, be determined by the degree to which the technology decreases greenhouse gas emissions, not by whether government has chosen to favor a particular technology. There is a danger that a program introduced as short-term could become permanent and grow in size, but that risk could be minimized by either taking these expenditures out of general revenues rather than earmarking allowances or tax revenues and/or including limitations in the authorizing legislation on their duration and size.

Price signals are also unlikely to reach fully the design of new vehicles, at least in the short run. Many car buyers do not take full account of the expense of fuel during the lifetime of the vehicle, because they are unaware of the cost, and may be even less aware of how a cap or tax on carbon emissions would increase that cost. For that reason, there should be a separate "cap" (or tax) on the carbon footprint of new vehicles, by which we mean the average greenhouse gas emissions per mile of new vehicles produced during the model year. Manufacturers could average the emissions of different models and trade allowances with other manufacturers, promoting flexibility and cost-effectiveness. With the adoption of this program, the current fuel economy standards would become redundant and should be eliminated.[21] Congress should allow states to choose between federal standards and the "California package" (stricter standards adopted by California and other states that adopt the same standards) with the proviso that this package allow trading within and between new vehicle fleets.

Similar reasoning raises concern about whether manufacturers of other items such as appliances will face adequate market demands from consumers to make them energy efficient. Here, as with vehicles, the federal government has a track record of requiring that products bear labels disclosing energy-efficiency information to consumers and also of directly regulating the energy efficiency of products.[22] The labeling requirements should be retained and strengthened. Energy efficiency standards requiring a specified performance level may also be warranted or a cap-and-trade or tax system. Such measures should take account of the costs of making products that use less energy and the economic and environmental benefits from lower energy use over the lifetime of the product. Decisions about which products should be subject to such measures should also consider the possibility that firms may use the regulatory system to thwart competitors and that consumers and manufacturers will lose desirable flexibility.

Price signals also fail to reach some choices influencing energy use that can be addressed by state and local policy tools such as public utility regulation, land use and transportation planning, and building codes. A price signal will not necessarily influence an apartment building owner's decision on how to insulate a building when it is tenants who pay for the heating and cooling. Similarly, a government authority may make land-use decisions that increase urban sprawl without taking into account the increase in gasoline usage it causes. These policy tools have traditionally been wielded by states and their subdivisions, which are better equipped than is the federal government to use them to increase energy efficiency.

The federal government should require states to adopt energy efficiency plans but should not try to regulate their content. This suggestion comes from a project participant, William Pedersen, who rose through the ranks of the EPA to become its deputy general counsel, and who is now a noted scholar and practicing attorney. The federal plan requirement would call states' attention to opportunities for reducing their energy use, but the states should be encouraged to pursue that possibility through the carrot of federal grants rather than the stick of federal regulation. Federal regulation of the contents of state energy plans is likely to be no more successful than were the federal government's failed attempts under the Clean Air Act in the 1970s to force the states to adopt plans to reduce driving.[23] Instead, the federal government should use grants to reward states that move in the right direction, with the reward based on measured accomplishments rather than promises of future success. It would be analytically and politically difficult to gauge the future impact of state promises in plans and comparatively easier to measure observed changes in energy efficiency within each state. The measurement could be done by keeping track of changes in energy usage per capita and per unit of economic activity. Congress would need to fund a federal office to do the measurement and develop appropriate grant formulae.

Congress should also require significant greenhouse gas sources to report their emissions and large buildings to report their energy usage.[24] Emissions from sources should be estimated by consistent, reliable means. This would aid the development and implementation of the state plans, bring opportunities for economies to the attention of the owners of these sources and buildings, and put pressure on them from consumers, investors, and others concerned with the environment.

Recommendations on Climate Change

To address climate change, Congress should:

- Enact a cap-and-trade (or, possibly, a tax) program limiting greenhouse gas emissions.

  One cap (or tax program) would apply to emissions from large stationary sources and fuels. There would be credits and offsets for any sources of emissions or sinks not covered by the program, including agriculture and forestry, as long as they can be adequately quantified and other reasonable regulatory conditions can be met.

  A second, separate cap (or tax program) would apply to greenhouse gas emissions from new vehicles.

  Energy-efficiency labeling and regulatory measures should be applied to selected products.

- Require states to adopt plans to conserve energy through reforms to current systems of public utility regulation, land use and transportation planning, building codes, and other state or local policy tools. The federal government should not control the contents of the state plans. It should instead reward success by providing states with grants based on each state's measured impact on energy use.

- Require reports on greenhouse emissions from large sources and energy usage from large buildings.

- Exclude greenhouse gas emissions from current Clean Air Act programs following adoption of a cap-and-trade (or, possibly, a tax) program for those emissions.

To keep the regulatory system current, Congress should:

- Establish a process to periodically reconsider the goals and methods of programs for regulating greenhouse gases in light of changes in knowledge and circumstances.

These recommendations accord with our four principles:

Principle 1: New regulatory tools as complements for traditional hierarchical regulation. To reduce emissions and encourage energy efficiency, our recommendations place primary reliance on market-based mechanisms such as cap and trade or taxes, supplemented by information disclosure.

Principle 2: Realignment of federal and state responsibilities. The federal government rather than the states would take the laboring oar, because climate change is an international problem. The state energy efficiency plans would, however, give a role to the states and local governments in areas where they have a comparative advantage. The rules on preemption would allow states to continue to take new initiatives to limit emissions from stationary sources. State regulation of nationally marketed goods such as vehicles raises special issues to be discussed in Chapter 5.

Principle 3: Trade-offs faced openly on the basis of reliable information. In setting the level of a cap or tax, Congress would inescapably have to face the trade-off between reducing greenhouse gas emissions and the economic and other consequences of doing so.

Principle 4: Crosscutting regulatory approaches. To the extent that the cap-and-trade or tax program does not cover activities that emit greenhouse gases or capture and sequester them, especially agriculture and forestry practices, a system of credits would take advantage of the opportunities they present. The credits would encourage forestation and better environmental management of forestry and agriculture, producing additional ecological benefits.

CHAPTER 5

Air Pollution
The Old Body

Andre Agassi was born in 1970 and became a tennis star in 1990 by reaching the finals of the French Open and the U.S. Open. He went on to win many important titles and, by virtue of a relentless conditioning program, kept winning them past the age most players retire from the world circuit. Conditioning can help an aging athlete maintain endurance and strength but may be less effective in maintaining joints, tendons, and ligaments. One reason is that tissue gets stiffer and more prone to injury over the years.[1] Agassi was forced to retire in 2006 at the age of thirty-six.

The Clean Air Act, too, is old and stiff. The statute, as we know it, took shape in 1970, the same year that Agassi was born, and was substantially updated but not fundamentally restructured in 1977 and again in 1990, the year that Agassi became a star. The many and detailed duties that the statute imposes make it especially prone to the inflexibility that comes with age. The word "shall" in the sense of signifying a duty is directed against the EPA administrator some 940 times and against states, governors, and others some 369 times. Many of these duties are triggered repeatedly. The duties are specified in such detail that the statute is 450 pages long. Over the years, they have been further elaborated in numerous court decisions.[2]

Such constraints under various statutes prompted William

Andre Agassi, U.S. Open, 1990. AP Images.

Andre Agassi, U.S. Open, 2006. AP Images.

Ruckelshaus to write, "The people who run EPA are not so much executives as prisoners of the stringent legislative mandates and court decisions that have been laid down like archeological strata for the past quarter-century."[3] This was written in 1995, yet the Clean Air Act has not been updated since 1990 (and even this updating did not fundamentally change the 1970 structure), despite the major differences between the air pollution challenges of today and those of 1990, let alone 1970. For a statute of its ambition and pervasive impact on the dynamic economic and environmental fabric of the country, the Clean Air Act is a remarkably old and inflexible body of law.

The imperative to enact climate legislation creates the need and the opportunity to revise the Clean Air Act's treatment of the most widespread pollutants, those subject to National Ambient Air Quality Standards ("criteria pollutants," including sulfur dioxide, nitrogen oxides, and particulate matter). The need arises because efforts to reduce greenhouse gases and criteria pollutants will clash unless Congress changes how the Clean Air Act regulates criteria pollutants. The opportunity arises because the changes needed to avoid this clash could also address important shortcomings in the act's ability to achieve further cuts in criteria pollutants. The most important shortcoming is the act's reliance on cumbersome state implementation plans to conscript states in regulating factories and other stationary sources. Far more effective in reducing pollution would be direct federal market-based regulation of the small fraction of stationary sources that account for the lion's share of stationary source pollution.

Unless the Clean Air Act is reformed, reductions in criteria pollutants generated as a co-benefit by the greenhouse gas cap-and-trade program will be lost, and the existing system for regulating criteria pollutants will impair the flexibility and efficiency of the climate cap-and-trade system.

The same sources, including power plants and major industrial facilities, generate both types of pollutants from the same fossil-fuel combustion processes. As a consequence, steps to cut emissions of the most important greenhouse gas, carbon dioxide, will cut emissions of combustion-related criteria pollutants as a co-benefit. A utility that replaces a coal-fired power plant with wind farms or nuclear power eliminates not only carbon dioxide emissions but also criteria pollutants that come from burning coal. So, too, a utility that makes its coal-fired plant more fuel efficient would reduce the two kinds of pollutants at once.

The current Clean Air Act's system for regulating criteria pollutants needs to be changed to ensure that this co-benefit is preserved. Otherwise, it will be squandered, as William Pedersen has shown. Consider what would happen when some sources complying with a requirement to cut greenhouse gas emissions also cut criteria pollutant emissions as a co-benefit. This co-benefit would mean that states could revise their state implementation plans to allow increases in criteria emissions from other sources without running afoul of the requirement that sources collectively achieve the National Ambient Air Quality Standards. Similar increases would occur under the cap-and-trade program for acid rain (which targets sulfur dioxide emissions) and several other cap-and-trade programs for certain pollutants to be mentioned later in this chapter. Sources cutting criteria pollutant emissions as a co-benefit of reducing greenhouse gas emissions would free up room under the cap to allow other sources to increase emissions. So, too, under the current program of emission controls from new vehicles, which allows each manufacturer to average emissions from its vehicle fleet, a manufacturer making models with zero criteria pollutant emissions as a co-benefit of reducing greenhouse gas emissions would be allowed to increase criteria pollutant emissions from other models.[4] In each of these instances, the cuts in criteria pollutants that come as a co-benefit would allow slacking off from the level of effort for controlling criteria pollutants now required under the Clean Air Act and, as a consequence, could wipe out environmental progress that would otherwise be made.

The failure to take advantage of the co-benefit, although perfectly legal under the current statute, would be a real loss to protection of the public health and the environment. National Ambient Air Quality Standards, caps, and other limits on emissions are generally not a magic dividing line between harm and safety. In practice, if not in theory, they represent a pragmatic judgment about a reasonable level of effort to control pollution.[5] We should change the current Clean Air Act in order to prevent sources from using the co-benefit from greenhouse gas controls to reduce efforts to control criteria pollutants. We should maintain that level of effort, plus get the additional cuts in criteria pollutants that come from controlling greenhouse gases, by coordinating the two regulatory systems. Dealing with climate change is no reason to allow sources to do less in controlling criteria pollutants.

A second aspect of the clash is that the methods that the Clean Air Act uses to control criteria pollutants would frustrate the efficient functioning of a cap or tax program to control greenhouse gases. As already explained, cap and trade or taxes can be efficient because either would give individual sources latitude to decide the amount to be cut and how. By establishing a cap reduction or tax schedule over a number of years, they also provide sources with the advance information needed to make the most of that latitude in their long-term research and investment plans. In contrast, many current Clean Air Act programs regulate the same combustion processes in the same sources in ways that not only constrain which sources make the cuts but often impact how a source makes them (see box on page 79). Moreover, the Clean Air Act changes those requirements frequently and in a piecemeal fashion, often pollutant by pollutant and program by program.[6] Such inflexible constraints and frequent changes not only make it more costly and difficult to reduce criteria pollutants efficiently but (because of the interdependency in measures to reduce different types of emissions from the same combustion processes) also interfere with the latitude and advance planning essential to efficiency in cutting greenhouse gases. We need an integrated, flexible approach to regulating both greenhouse gases and criteria pollutants that promotes innovation and the investments needed to deploy it.

Does the Clean Air Act Tell Sources How to Cut Pollution?

Under the Clean Air Act, EPA in many cases cannot directly require sources to use a particular control technology to limit emissions. To the contrary, the agency is to set performance standards limiting emissions, usually expressed not in terms of the absolute quantity of pollutant emitted but rather an emissions rate based on production process inputs or outputs—for example, no more than x lbs of y pollutant per million BTU of fuel input in a steam electric generating plant.[7] Sources are then supposed to have the flexibility to use whatever control technology or other method that allows them to achieve the performance standard. According to a National Research Council study, however, "Although the flexibility exists in theory, in practice the performance standard is normally set at the level that can most readily be achieved by a known technology. Thus, unless readily available alternatives can meet the standards to the satisfaction of regulators, there is likely to be a tendency to default to the known technology, thus avoiding options for the affected industries."[8]

The statute, as interpreted by EPA, also theoretically gives sources another sort of flexibility. Although it calls for regulators to set performance standards limiting emissions from the various industrial processes within a plant and often from specific smokestacks or vents, the source under some programs can total all the emissions of a pollutant emitted from different outlets in the plant and make this total rather than the separate outlet emissions the target for regulatory limits.[9] This approach, which places an imaginary "bubble" over all of the emissions from the plant, gives managers flexibility to target the emission reductions necessary to meet the overall limit on those processes and the points within the plant where they would cost least. Regulatory reality is, however, again more complicated. Different performance standards apply to different industrial processes, each pollutant can be regulated under multiple programs, and multiple pollutants are regulated. The multiplicity of requirements makes it difficult and sometimes legally or operationally impossible to implement the bubble approach and "can raise the cost of emissions control without adding any appreciable benefit in emissions reductions," according to a report by the National Research Council.[10] It goes on: "The result has been to make it difficult for any one facility to implement multipollutant controls in a systematic and cost-effective fashion."[11] Moreover, many of the separate regulatory requirements for different processes and outlets are formulated in terms of emissions rates specified in different terms over different averaging periods, compounding the practical difficulty of developing a common metric in order to operationalize the bubble approach. Also, regulators tend to impose tight restrictions on use of a rate-based bubble because it can be "gamed" by sources in ways that a bubble based on absolute emissions cannot.[12]

In sum, although the statute can be read to give sources a moderate degree of flexibility as to which points within their plants they can cut emissions and how, the reality is often to the contrary.

EPA could theoretically ameliorate one of these clashes—the squandering of the co-benefit at least in some places—by imposing new criteria pollutant controls, but doing so would exacerbate the other by further undercutting the efficiencies from a cap-and-trade or tax approach to greenhouse gases. The EPA has the authority under the Clean Air Act to examine each major new or modified stationary source and require it to stay within the emission rate achievable by using the cleanest technology workable in its individual circumstances. The agency could consider technologies that reduce the amount of combustion per unit of product as well as technologies that reduce the amount of pollution per unit of combustion. Imposing such an emission limit would tend to drive sources to adopt the technologies the agency has in mind. However, this in itself would not stop the squandering of the co-benefit, because the cuts from new or modified sources would allow existing sources to increase emissions by a corresponding amount. Yet, the EPA could do something in addition in some places. Where a National Ambient Air Quality Standard has not been achieved for a pollutant, EPA has authority to require existing sources to achieve emission limits using "reasonable available control technology," as the agency defines it, to control that pollutant. It could similarly use this authority to adopt requirements that will drive sources toward adopting the technologies the agency has in mind. By so doing, however, EPA would end up largely determining which sources should improve energy efficiency and otherwise control combustion processes and their criteria pollutants emissions, and how they should do so. But these specifications would also affect greenhouse gases emitted from the same sources. As a result, the agency would have superimposed a hierarchical regime upon a cap-and-trade or tax approach to greenhouse gas reduction, re-creating many of the inefficiencies of centralized planning that the adoption of market-based incentives was designed to avoid. And the co-benefit would still be squandered in regions where the National Ambient Air Quality Standards for a criteria pollutant have been attained because EPA lacks authority to control existing sources there.

Moreover, whatever its legal authority, EPA lacks the administrative resources to fine tune the regulation of criteria pollutants to avoid squandering the co-benefit. The perennial shortage of resources at EPA, already noted, will grow worse once Congress asks it to control greenhouse gases as well. The shortage of resources can, however, be alleviated by adopting a more streamlined method to achieve criteria pollutant objectives. We will shortly show how.

Furthermore, the Clean Air Act could discourage renovations of some existing plants. Renovations to improve energy efficiency are an environmentally and economically desirable way of cutting greenhouse gases. Such renovations can be discouraged by the current statutory requirement that any existing plant that undergoes a physical change resulting in a more than minimal increase in emissions of a pollutant is deemed a "modified" source and must meet the stricter emission-control requirements applicable to new or modified plants. A plant renovation to improve energy efficiency, even though it cuts emissions of greenhouse gases and many criteria pollutants, can result in the EPA's determining that the physical change would cause a sufficient increase in emissions in some other pollutant to trigger these requirements. Whether EPA will determine that a plant renovation triggers stricter pollution requirements is often unclear. A source that predicts the agency will judge its renovation to trigger the stricter emission control requirements could be deterred by the expense of meeting them. A source that predicts the contrary could be deterred by the uncertainty of its prediction. If it is wrong, the agency will require retrofits and penalties.[13]

The EPA could reduce the extent to which the stricter standards for modified plants would deter improvements by clarifying the method it uses to determine whether a physical change would cause a sufficient increase in emissions to trigger the stricter requirements and by making them more forgiving. That, however, would work against the purpose of imposing tougher standards through new and modified source programs, which is to drive down emissions over time. Our proposal would achieve that purpose through a cap-

and-trade program with declining caps on criteria pollutants. This program would achieve steady reductions but would not place stricter requirements on particular modified sources and so would not deter renovations to improve energy efficiency.

Once a greenhouse gas cap and trade program is adopted, the frequently changing requirements that the Clean Air Act generates for criteria pollutants would also force wasteful expenditures for their control. For example, state implementation plans require capital expenditures to achieve the National Ambient Air Quality Standard by a statutory deadline; such expenditures may also be required to stay within the declining cap under existing cap-and-trade programs for criteria pollutants. Yet, the equipment thus required could shortly become unnecessary to achieve the criteria standard or cap when the program to control greenhouse gases reduces criteria pollutants as a co-benefit. The result: equipment installed at considerable expense would soon go unused.[14] A capital expenditure with such a short-term benefit is simply wasteful, but such waste is what the current statute would require.

Independent of conflicts with greenhouse gas cap and trade, the Clean Air Act needs reform in order to achieve greater cuts in criteria pollutants through the use of network tools. The heart of the Clean Air Act, wrote the Supreme Court, is the requirement that states adopt implementation plans and control emission sources to achieve federally set air-quality standards by specified deadlines. Based on this requirement, Congress told voters in 1970, "all Americans in all parts of the country shall have clean air to breathe within the 1970s." Congress required that state implementation plans achieve the National Ambient Air Quality Standards to protect health by 1977 at the latest. The state implementations plans did improve air quality somewhat, but they did not come close to the air-quality standards by 1977. Indeed, air quality standards were still widely violated in 1990, and many regions have still not attained them.[15]

Much more successful, in contrast, were four provisions of the Clean Air Act that called upon the federal government to regulate sources directly rather than conscripting state regulators:

- In 1970, Congress required auto manufacturers to cut emissions from new cars by 90 percent. The most recent vehicles have achieved even greater cuts because of subsequent amendments and regulations.

- In 1970, Congress effectively mandated that motorists use lead-free gas in new cars, thus eventually eliminating by far the largest source of airborne lead.

- In 1990, Congress through the acid rain cap and trade program required that power plants cut their emissions of sulfur dioxide by 50 percent from 1980 levels by 2010. The cut was 43 per cent from 1990 levels by 2007.[16]

- In 1990, Congress adopted a ban or phase out of the production and use of most chemicals that harm stratospheric ozone. This has been accomplished.[17] The use of these chemicals has been eliminated or drastically reduced.

The state implementation process was less successful than direct federal regulation in part because of its elaborate bureaucratic procedures. EPA is responsible for ensuring that *each* state adopts and implements a plan to achieve the National Ambient Air Quality Standards for *each* pollutant in *each* of its air-quality control regions. Through this plenitude of plans, EPA must consider how the states deal with hundreds of thousands of stationary sources, tens of millions of drivers, local transportation planning, and more. Moreover, EPA must require the states to revise their plans in light of periodic changes in the National Ambient Air Quality Standards (mandated by the statute and enforced by litigation) and the many failures to achieve the air-quality standards on time. A 2004 National Research Council study found, in unusually strong language, that the state implementation plan process "now mandates extensive amounts of local, state, and federal agency time and resources in a legalistic, and often frustrating proposal and review process, which focuses primarily on compliance with intermediate process steps. This process probably discourages innovation and experimentation at the state and local levels; overtaxes the limited financial and human resources available to the nation's [air quality management] system at the state, local, and federal levels; and draws attention and resources away from the more germane issue of ensuring progress toward the goal of meeting the [National Ambient Air Quality Standards]."[18] So, while the state implementation process began with the laudable objective of assuring no place had unhealthy air quality, it has had, while doing some good, the unintended consequence of also getting in the way of improving air quality.

Another fundamental problem with the state implementation plan process is that it puts the states and the EPA in the politically awkward position of imposing different emission limits on different sources. The requirements in state plans are, by definition, not nationally applicable and, indeed, often vary from source to source in order to reduce the cost of achieving the federal ambient standards or to meet claims of hardship or inequity. Having to apportion the pollution reduction burden among particular sources often creates enormous pressure on the states and the EPA, putting regulators in a no-win dilemma. At the same time, the Clean Air Act imposes daunting penalties on states for failing to prepare plans that promise attainment of the National Ambient Air Quality Standards, but much slighter penalties for failing to *deliver* on the promises—penalties that are seldom enforced. It is not surprising that state plans often fail to cut emissions sufficiently to achieve the National Ambient Air Quality Standards.[19] By contrast, under cap and trade, the allocation of abatement burdens among individual sources is made through the impersonal market, and the cap ensures that reduction targets are achieved.

Still another problem with the state implementation plan process is that it discourages flexible alternatives to traditional hierarchical regulation that can better achieve further reductions once the low-hanging fruit has been plucked. In contrast, the four successful programs of direct federal regulation cited above relied upon cap and trade and other forms of regulation that have flexibility as their common characteristic. For one example, the acid rain cap-and-trade program allowed trading from the outset. For another example, the regulation of new cars took a traditional form at first, with each car having to meet a specified standard, but EPA later regulated the average emissions of each manufacturer's fleet, which functionally allowed trading within the fleets.[20] The move to more flexibility predictably followed from the increasing difficulty of achieving successively lower emission limits. Trading provided the flexibility needed to overcome this increasing difficulty.

Although traditional hierarchical regulation through state implementation plans has produced some significant success in cutting criteria pollutants, it has already done what it can do readily. Further progress requires steps that are tougher for traditional regulation to find, much more complex and costly, and more politically controversial.

The same logic that recommends cap and trade for controlling greenhouse gases, and that overcame the increasing difficulty of wringing greater reductions in emissions from new vehicles, now recommends cap and trade for reducing criteria pollutant emissions from major stationary sources. Cap and trade would use market forces to stimulate development of innovative technologies, search out the sources that can make the cuts most economically, and target the investments there. That is why Congress adopted cap and trade in 1990 to address acid rain, and why the EPA opted for cap and trade in two important rules. One, the 1998 "NOx SIP Call," imposed a cap-and-trade program on a few pollutants from one category of source in one region. The second, the 2005 "Clean Air Interstate Rule," extended the coverage of this program, but it was still only in one region, applied to only one category of source, and applied to only some criteria pollutants.[21]

The Clean Air Act puts many impediments in the way of trading between sources within a single state and even more impediments to trading between states.[22] Yet, trading brings the greatest benefits to the environment and the economy when regulation does not place extraneous limits on trading and sources are allowed to trade across the nation, or at least regionally, and across source categories. Only then does the market achieve the greatest cost savings and produce the maximum stimulus to innovate and achieve the smartest moves in cutting more pollution for less cost. Greater reduction of emissions at lower cost is a key virtue in our current time of financial trouble and tight resources.

A fresh reminder that the old statute sharply limits the ability of regulators to use network tools rather than hierarchical regulation came when the court of appeals decided in 2008 that the Clean Air Interstate Rule conflicts with the Clean Air Act. The decision was to the regret of regulators, industry, and environmental groups. The court remanded that rule to the agency to cure the conflicts.[23] At this writing, it is at best unclear whether EPA can cure these conflicts consistent with the court opinion and still maintain a viable cap-and-trade program. Existing cap-and-trade programs apply to only some criteria pollutants, from a limited range of pollution sources, and (except for the acid rain program) in limited regions. To achieve the maximum environmental and economic benefit, cap and trade must apply to all criteria pollutants, from all important sources, and in all regions.

Here is our proposal to meet the need and seize the opportunity. Congress should adopt direct federal controls, largely market-based, on the relatively small number of large sources that produce the lion's share of criteria pollutant emissions and link these controls to those of the federal program regulating greenhouse gases. These direct federal controls, rather than the roundabout, process-heavy state implementation plans, should be the centerpiece of the effort to achieve the National Ambient Air Quality Standards and other national air-quality objectives.

Before describing this proposal more fully, we pause to note that it would address the problems in the current Clean Air Act identified above. It would not squander the co-benefit, would avoid requiring unnecessary investment in capital equipment, and would eliminate the chief ways that the current highly hierarchical regime for regulating criteria pollutants would thwart the innovation and efficiencies that could otherwise be produced by a market-based approach to greenhouse gases. Allowing much more trading in the control of criteria pollutants would achieve greater reductions than are now possible. Finally, it would be a vastly simpler system for EPA, the states, and regulated sources to administer.

Our proposal entails four steps. The program as a whole should ensure reductions in criteria pollutants that are substantially greater than those that could and would realistically be achieved under the current Clean Air Act system.[24]

(1) Adopt direct federal controls on all important sources of criteria pollutants, including large stationary sources, fuels, and new vehicles. These controls should to the maximum extent feasible, be cap-and-trade.

Congress should institute direct federal regulation of emissions from the largest stationary sources and continue direct federal regulation of emissions from new motor vehicles, fuels, and paints and solvents, all of which are nationally marketed products.[25]

Cap and trade should be used whenever feasible, including for major stationary sources. As for new vehicles, the federal regulation could take the form of a limit on average emissions per vehicle. Manufacturers should be able to average emissions of the vehicles in their fleets for each model year and trade with other manufacturers. A parallel approach should apply to paints, solvents, and fuels.[26] If there are source categories whose emissions cannot be measured or reliably estimated, they should be subject to federal emission limits without trading, but also expressed in terms that maximize the flexibility of sources to choose the means to achieve those limits.

In the case of cap and trade, Congress should prescribe how the caps shall decline over time and how to apportion allowances, preferably by auction.[27] If political feasibility requires issuing some free allowances, this should be for a limited period of time. Moreover, allowances should be allocated on the basis of units of output, rather than units of input (in order to encourage efficiency) or on historical emissions (in order not to fence out new entrants). In the case of any other federal regulations, Congress should similarly lay down the rules prescribing how much emissions should be cut over time and apportioning the cleanup burdens.

The schedule of emission reductions for criteria pollutants should be expressly linked to and coordinated with the emissions-reduction schedule for greenhouse gases, so as to take advantage of the co-benefit described earlier and to avoid requiring the installation of control equipment that would become obsolete in a few years. In the case of source categories subject to trading for criteria pollutants, this link should take the form of a system of safety-valve prices, which would work as follows.[28] To guard against sources slacking off on criteria pollutant controls as a result of steps to reduce greenhouse gas emissions or as a result of unexpected breakthroughs in control technology, the number of allowances for a criteria pollutant should be decreased if their market price falls below a set level. To guard against sources having to install equipment that soon becomes unnecessary or against unexpected difficulties in controlling criteria pollutants, the number of allowances should be increased if the market price rises above another set level.

These safety-valve prices, coordinated with the greenhouse gas cap, would determine the level of criteria pollutant control effort required from industry. As pollution control techniques become more efficient and the price of allowances drops, the cap would keep dropping to maintain the level of effort, with no set end point. In other words, pollution levels would keep going down through sustained market-based incentives applicable to all sources rather than through the current act's mechanism of subjecting new or modified sources to stricter emission limits than existing sources. The current act's approach produces much less pollution reduction for the money.[29]

For source categories not regulated by cap and trade, the danger would be having to make investments that would soon be unnecessary. To guard against that, sources should be allowed to postpone compliance with the emission limit for a limited period by paying a set fee.[30]

We do not recommend any basic changes in the current system of regulation for especially hazardous air pollutants.[31]

(2) Select those stationary sources to be subjected to direct federal control to maximize the portion of criteria pollution covered and to minimize the federal administrative burden.

The stationary sources to be subjected to direct federal control should be selected with the twin objectives of maximizing federal control of pollution and reducing the administrative burden at the federal level to manageable proportions. The EPA's list of pollution sources includes 52,194 "point sources" in 874 categories, plus hundreds of thousands of generally much smaller "area sources." Consider, instead, by way of illustration, direct federal control over sources in only twelve categories: power plants, electric and other services combined, petroleum refiners, paper mills, hydraulic cement mills, pulp mills, organic chemical plants, primary aluminum plants, carbon black plants, blast furnaces, lead smelters, and raw sugar mills. In that case, federal regulation would cover only 3,225 point sources—that is, 6 percent of the point sources and 0 percent of the area sources.[32] Yet, together with continued regulation of new vehicles, fuels, and paints and solvents, direct federal regulation would deal with the great majority of ambient concentrations covered by criteria pollutants, as shown in table 2.

Table 2. Portion of Emissions That Would Be Federally Controlled

Pollutant	Portion Federally Regulated
Sulfur dioxide	85 percent
Nitrogen oxides	84 percent
Volatile organic compounds	Over 75 percent
Particulate matter	Over 75 percent
Carbon monoxide	83 percent
Lead	By far the largest source, lead additives to vehicular gasoline have been eliminated. Two-thirds of the remaining lead emissions would be covered.

SOURCE: David Schoenbrod, Joel Schwartz & Ross Sandler, "Air Pollution: Building on the Successes," 17 *New York University Environmental Law Journal* 284, 301–4 (2008).

These numbers are based upon treating vehicle emissions as federally controlled, because the federal government has regulated and would continue to regulate emissions from new vehicles. Yet, new vehicles replace old ones slowly, especially in the case of trucks and other heavy equipment. Older versions of such equipment are significant sources of pollution. Consideration should be given to supplementing the federal controls proposed with a market-based federal program to retrofit such equipment.

These numbers understate the degree to which *controllable* pollution would be subject to direct federal regulation. Some emissions not covered by our proposal come from sources that are impossible to control, such as accidental fires in forests or buildings. Almost all of the rest come from sources that are individually smaller, including substantial facilities that produce only modest emissions and small enterprises and residences. Many of these sources have never been regulated under state implementation plans. For example, the Clean Air Act has not, in four decades of operation, brought about controls on house space heaters or hot water heaters in most of the country and is unlikely to do so in the any time soon.[33] The obstacles in control costs, administrative resources, and political pain are just too great.

Our proposal should be refined to increase the proportion of controllable emissions subject to federal control without appreciably increasing the federal administrative burden. EPA has the capability and the raw data on individual sources to suggest additional large sources that should be subject to direct federal control and smaller sources that could be omitted from it without an appreciable impact on air quality.[34]

(3) Set these federal controls to achieve national air-quality goals rather than relying primarily on state implementation plans.

Our proposal would produce an ever renewing, long-term reduction in criteria pollutant emissions through economic incentives that would drive technical progress and reap all the co-benefits of increasingly tight greenhouse gas controls. Congress should set the required level of effort so as to first achieve national air-quality goals on a schedule that is cost-effective and consistent with the greenhouse gas control effort. Where necessary, regional caps should be set to, for example, protect visibility in national parks. EPA has staff and data that Congress could call upon to do the analytic work needed to assemble this new regulatory program.[35]

Meanwhile, the state implementation plan process and its related programs should be reduced to a backstop role, as described below.

(4) Establish backstops in the federal system of direct regulation to deal with backsliding, harmful interstate spillovers, hot spots, or shortfalls in achieving National Ambient Air Quality Standards.

The legislation should contain safeguard provisions to deal with problems that could arise if the direct federal controls including cap and trade fail to produce the expected emission reductions or if some states fail to regulate small sources adequately. Underlying these provisions would be a universal requirement that states generate, make publicly available, and report to EPA accurate information on sources' emissions, aggregate emissions inventories, and air quality, and that these information provisions be enforceable through citizen suits.

If the cap-and-trade approach fails to produce the predicted emissions reductions on schedule, or if these reductions do not lead to the predicted air-quality benefits, EPA should be required to take corrective action by, for example, tightening cap requirements, establishing regional caps, or supplementing the cap with selected source-by-source controls.

A state's backsliding in controlling emissions from small stationary sources not subject to the federal system might interfere with attaining national air-quality goals. The appropriate response is a federal backstop to be invoked if and when required. Should a state allow total emissions from sources left to its control to increase above baseline levels, it would have to adopt and enforce a state implementation plan to eliminate the excess. An exception should be allowed when state-regulated sources buy sufficient emission allowances from federally regulated sources to offset the increased emissions; this will ensure offsetting reductions from other sources. States will be anxious to avoid the burdens of the implementation plan process, so this backstop may be triggered only infrequently. Where such a plan is necessary, it need only apply to sources not subject to direct federal control, and so would not interfere significantly with the federal programs of direct regulation.

By failing to regulate adequately sources under its controls, a state can also cause harmful spillovers in a downwind state. Such spillovers would be much less likely under our proposals than under existing law because there would be federal controls on the great majority of controllable emissions, and the portion left to the states would tend to come from sources without tall smokestacks. Nonetheless, a backstop should be provided and can be structured that so that it is far more useable than the authority under present law.[36]

As the acid rain program demonstrates, the cost effectiveness of cap and trade makes it feasible to achieve deeper cuts in emissions than under traditional hierarchical regulation. Deeper reductions go a long way toward reducing the risk of hot spots, because overall average ambient concentrations will be lower. In particular, with the caps continuing to drop with no end point, there would be continuing economic pressure on both new and existing sources everywhere to adopt the best practices available and for the dirtier existing sources to be replaced.

Not only would cap and trade do a better job of reducing aggregate emissions, but there is little reason to suppose that it will exacerbate regional differentials in emissions. The acid rain trading program achieved the largest reductions in the part of the country with the highest levels of pollution. Based upon such findings, the National Research Council's 2004 report on pollution control concluded that trading is unlikely to create hot spots, but in the unlikely event that it does, steps could be taken to "guard against even the possibility."[37] The report mentioned regional caps, where needed, and proposed allowing states to impose their own tougher regulations—both of which we endorse.

We recommend as an additional safeguard that the federal trading scheme ban any existing federally regulated source from increasing emissions of criteria pollutants above current baseline levels by more than a minimal amount, except upon showing that this would not violate the National Ambient Air Quality Standards.[38]

Finally, the hot spot concern focuses most prominently on especially hazardous pollutants. Of course, some criteria pollutants such as particulate matter include many different chemicals, some of which are themselves quite hazardous. EPA can and does regulate these components under the Clean Air Act's provision dealing with especially hazardous pollutants, and we do not propose any changes in this authority.

Even if federal controls on federally regulated sources are tightened in response to a failure to achieve national air-quality goals, as discussed above, it may be that state controls on small sources remain so weak as to prevent achievement of those goals in one or a few states. If this occurs, state implementation plan requirements could be imposed for such states.

The first line of preventive defense against the contingencies addressed by these backstops is the states themselves. To help the states do a better job, Congress should require the EPA to issue suggested guidelines to states and localities on options for regulating sources not subject to direct federal control. In addition, as discussed in Chapter 3, EPA should, based on the public emissions and air-quality information, rank states' and localities' performance in controlling these sources in order to make them more accountable to their citizens.[39]

Finally, Congress should not preempt states from imposing tougher controls on federally regulated stationary sources. As to new vehicles, Congress should allow states to choose between federal standards and the "California package" with the proviso that these California controls allow trading within and between new vehicle fleets.[40]

Our proposal would equip federal regulators with all the tools needed to achieve national air-quality goals. With expanded direct federal regulation, including a broadly applicable cap-and-trade program with a continually declining cap, and backup safeguards, it would no longer be necessary or worthwhile to shoulder the burdens, costs, and delays associated with a state implementation plan and related program requirements imposed by the current Clean Air Act. These requirements should be dropped or modified, as described in the box on page 95.

Streamlining Criteria Pollutant Regulation

Inspection and maintenance. The Clean Air Act requires implementation plans in many states to mandate "inspection and maintenance" of light-duty vehicles. Empirical studies suggest that the program reduces pollution little, if at all, despite costing large sums and inconveniencing tens of millions of motorists. Recent changes in federal requirements to trim this burden will make the program even less effective but not much less burdensome. This requirement should be eliminated, or, at the minimum, states should be given far more flexibility in achieving its purposes.[41]

Transportation conformity. Another component of the state implementation plan requirement is that state transportation officials show that their federally funded transportation projects are consistent with achieving the National Ambient Air Quality Standards. Yet it costs tens to hundreds of times more to avoid a ton of emissions through transportation infrastructure decisions than through direct emission limits on vehicles.[42] Transportation conformity is not a cost-effective way to protect air quality. Of course, there are many reasons other than air quality to be concerned about transportation infrastructure, including energy efficiency, climate change, and sprawl. The federal interest in those decisions can be realized through the recommendation for state energy efficiency plans that would include land use and transportation planning, as outlined in Chapter 4.

Significant deterioration and enhanced visibility. Still another component of the state implementation plan requirement is that states prevent "significant deterioration" of air quality in regions that have achieved the National Ambient Air Quality Standards. This program serves to minimize increases in pollution, particularly in areas near great national parks. Other provisions of the Clean Air Act seek to protect and enhance visibility in such areas. The purposes of these programs would be better served by our proposal. The cap-and-trade program would impose a declining cap on emissions of criteria pollutants and thus is a powerful tool to minimize emissions. Regional caps could produce especially clean air and enhance visibility surrounding these parks. The sources we recommend for direct federal control include the source categories targeted in current visibility enhancement efforts.[43]

New Source Review. As part of the implementation plan process, major new or modified sources must undergo New Source Review if they increase their emissions more than a set amount. One feature of this program is to vet such sources. This feature should be retained as a tool to enforce the backstop provisions discussed in the text above. Another feature of New Source Review, which requires new or modified sources to meet tougher emission limits than existing sources, should be scrapped. This feature, as already noted, can interfere with incentives for plant modifications to increase energy efficiency and reduce greenhouse gas emissions. Moreover, cap and trade can achieve much greater emission reductions than New Source Review for the same expense. According to a 2006 analysis of power plant data by the National Research Council, "A national market-based trading program with emission caps below those specified by [Clean Air Interstate Rule] could produce emission reductions at approximately *one third or less of the cost* of aggressive implementation of the prerevision [New Source Review] rules."[44]

New Source Performance Standards. Like New Source Review, New Source Performance Standards impose tougher requirements on new or modified stationary sources than ordinarily applied to existing ones.[45] The stated objective was to reduce emissions as plants are replaced, but as with New Source Review, cap and trade is a better way to achieve this objective.

As in the case of greenhouse gases, changes in knowledge or circumstances may make the reformed Clean Air Act that we propose inadequate to achieve national objectives. We have already proposed a process for regular review and, if needed, changes in the greenhouse gas program. That process should also provide for EPA or another expert body to analyze and propose to Congress the following: needed changes in the levels of National Ambient Air Quality Standards; which sources will be federally regulated; the caps on federally regulated sources; and the various fallback safeguards.

Recommendations on Air Pollution Regulation

Simultaneously with enacting the program to deal with climate change, Congress should also reform the Clean Air Act's framework for regulating conventional air pollution to:

- Adopt direct federal controls on all important sources of criteria pollutants, including large stationary sources, fuels, and new vehicles.

    These direct federal controls should take the form of cap and trade.

    Congress should set the caps to decline over time, determine the method of distributing the allowances, and expressly link these federal controls to the cap-and-trade or tax program on greenhouse gases.

- Set the emission reduction schedule of these direct federal controls to achieve national air-quality goals at the pace set by Congress rather than through state implementation plans and related programs, including New Source Review, New Source Performance Standards, vehicle inspection and maintenance, and transportation conformity requirements.

- Establish backstops to remedy any failure of the federal cap-and-trade system to perform as expected; any backsliding by states or harmful interstate spillovers; hot spots; or shortfalls in achieving National Ambient Air Quality Standards.

- Require EPA to provide the states and localities with guidelines for regulating the small sources of predominantly intrastate pollution left to their control and to provide the public with candid rankings of states' and localities' performance in reducing emissions and improving air quality.

To keep the regulatory system current, Congress should:

- Establish a process to periodically reconsider the goals and methods of the program for regulating criteria pollutants in light of changes in knowledge and circumstances, in conjunction with the process to reconsider the programs dealing with greenhouse gas programs.

These recommendations accord with our four principles:

Principle 1: New regulatory tools as complements for traditional hierarchical regulation. Our recommendations maximize the use of market-based mechanisms consistent with concerns about hot spots and administrative feasibility. They also use information-based mechanisms to improve state regulation.

Principle 2: Realignment of federal and state responsibilities. The federal government would finally get direct control of those sources that make the biggest contribution to interstate pollution. States would be left free to regulate the far larger number of much smaller sources, subject to federal safeguards that are unlikely to be often needed.

Principle 3: Trade-offs faced openly on the basis of reliable information. Congress would inescapably have to face the trade-offs in setting the caps on emissions and the other federal emission limits.

Principle 4: Crosscutting regulatory approaches. Control of criteria pollutants would be integrated with the other environmental problem with which it is most intimately connected, climate change.

CHAPTER 6

Lands, Waters, and Other Natural Resources
The Organized Ant

Army ants go forth to hunt in hordes of hundreds of thousands. "Wherever they move," a naturalist wrote in 1863, "the whole animal world is set in commotion, and every creature tries to get out of their way." What gives the ants such power is self-organization, which allows them to act collectively. Through collective action,

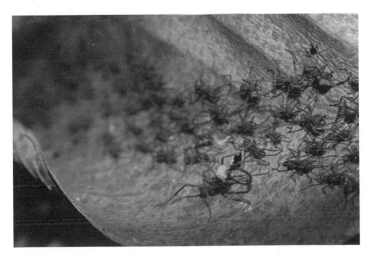

A raiding column of the army ant *Eciton burchellii* in the Brazilian Amazon rain forest. Photo: Daniel Kronauer.

these tiny ants can take on prey that tower over them, such as crickets and cockroaches, and even sometimes vertebrates.[1]

The power of collective action also figures in fights among humans over who benefits from government-owned natural resources. When Congress gives agencies broad power to decide between the claims of competing uses such as logging and hiking, the agencies tend to favor uses advocated by people who are well organized and therefore better able to work collectively to bring pressure on the government. Through collective action, a well-organized interest group can sometimes persuade an agency to let it use the resource even though the benefits to the special interest are small compared to the harm done to the public at large. An example is the failure of federal agencies to stop ranchers from grazing so many head of livestock on public lands that vegetation is nibbled to the ground, soil erodes into streams, species disappear, and the land looks like hell. The grazing on vast tracts of public lands produces only 2 percent of the nation's meat. Yet the grazing wins out in large part because ranchers are organized into trade associations, and businesses that service them are organized into local and regional chambers of commerce. In contrast, only a tiny fraction of citizens who lose because of the abuse of public lands belong to organizations dedicated to preventing the destruction.[2]

The return from grazing is so meager in some places that nonprofit conservation groups supported by only a small subset of the public can afford to pay enough to persuade ranchers to part with their permits to graze on public land. One such group, the Grand Canyon Trust, purchased from ranchers their permits to graze livestock in the Grand Staircase Escalante National Monument in southern Utah. The trust then asked the Bureau of Land Management to amend its plan so as to retire the land from grazing.[3] The sellers, one of whom was the county commissioner, and the local bureau office supported the request.

This request would, one might predict, get quickly approved. The ranchers got a price that they willingly accepted, and grazing would stop in a national monument area. Where grazing has stopped altogether, the land, although still bearing marks of past abuse, improves dramatically. Moreover, as John Leshy and Molly McUsic tell the story, "The local Congressman, Chris Cannon, wrote Interior Secretary Gale Norton to urge her 'to support this worthwhile effort.' Norton, who had advocated 'free market' solutions earlier in her career when she worked for the conservative, market-oriented Mountain States Legal Foundation, responded that she 'strongly endorsed this action,' because 'this type of market-based solution can provide an excellent opportunity for local groups to work together to benefit the community and the land.' "[4]

The prediction that the request would be quickly approved, however, fails to account for the power of collective action. Opposition to retiring permits often comes from other ranchers who want the permits to expand their own operations, local businesses whose revenues come from supplying ranchers, and ranching trade associations whose power would diminish if there were fewer ranchers. Such forces showed impressive organization in the case of the Grand Staircase Escalante National Monument permits. Leshy and McUsic continue: "According to Interior Department sources who must remain confidential, the entire Utah congressional delegation, including Congressman Cannon, came to oppose the retirement, as did every single commissioner in the two counties involved—including even the rancher-commissioner who had sold his grazing permits to the Trust. The Secretary bowed to the pressure and ordered [the Bureau of Land Management] to postpone work on the plan amendment."[5]

The bureau has still, after many years, never decided whether to retire the land from grazing.[6] That means that if the Grand Canyon Trust stops grazing on this land or other public lands on which it has purchased permits, its permits could be canceled and new permits on the same lands given to other ranchers in the vicinity. To avoid this depressing outcome, the Trust had to set up a ranching subsidiary that negotiates with the government on how *few* cattle it must graze to avoid forfeiting the permits. Yet the Trust does not want to be in the cattle business at all, and the land will not recover as well if it continues to be grazed.

Leshy and McUsic propose that Congress enact a statute that entitles the holder of a grazing permit to retire it.[7] This means that a rancher-seller and a land preservation group-buyer would have the power to agree on a purchase that would result in retiring the grazing permit. The ranchers will be most prone to sell permits on the least productive land; the preservation groups will be most apt to buy permits on ecologically sensitive and important lands.

The Leshy-McUsic proposal has three features designed to solve the general problem, of which overgrazing is an example, of how to get fairer consideration of uses of public resources, such as preservation and conservation, that are often at an organizational disadvantage to other uses, especially exploitative ones.

One feature of the Leshy-McUsic proposal is to shift the decision from a low-visibility forum (in the overgrazing example, a planning decision about a particular tract of land by a federal agency) to a higher visibility forum (consideration in Congress of a statute about a question of broad principle, in this case whether nonprofit purchasers of grazing permits should be able to retire them).[8] The superior organization of the ranching interests still gives them an advantage in Congress, but not nearly as much as before the agency whose action is unlikely to attract much attention in the national press and where elected legislators do not have to take a position in public. This feature is an application of the principle in favor of facing trade-offs in the open.

A second feature is to use the carrot of cash payments for grazing permits rather than the stick of agency regulations restricting permit use, much as the carrot of cash payments from selling offsets would get farmers and forest owners to change practices in ways that increase sequestration of carbon. One might argue that it is wrong to pay ranchers to stop hurting public lands, given that the statute under which the permits were issued gives the government the right to revoke them.[9] The ranchers, on the other hand, might argue that the permits have long been treated as if they are property—handed down through the generations in wills, bought and sold between ranchers, and mortgaged. Rather than engaging in an argument of principle, the Leshy-McUsic proposal takes as its starting point the proposition that decades of effort to secure tighter regulation have not worked and, while not giving up on regulation, turns to purchases as a complementary way to protect more land.

The third feature is to shift some aspects of control of the natural resource from a regulatory agency to private decisionmakers, such as a rancher holding a permit and buyers such as nonprofit groups that may wish to retire it. The agency is subject to the power of the highly organized interests that want to stop retirement of grazing permits, but the individual rancher who owns a permit and the buyer who wants to retire it are not. Thus, the shift in power of decision, once accomplished, negates the superior political organization of ranching interests. By shifting the locus of decision, the second and third features skirt the obstacles created by hierarchical regulation and take advantage of network tools for environmental protection.

The political scientist Elinor Ostrom, an expert on the governance of resources held in common, argues that there are three basic approaches: the resource can be privatized, managed by the government, or managed by a community of resource users.[10] There are many variations on these basic approaches (if government is to manage, the decisions might be made by a legislature or an agency and at the federal, state, or local level). Hybrid approaches are also possible, as the Leshy-McUsic proposal illustrates.

There is no one right design for the management of natural resources. Rather, the challenge is to come up with the approach most apt to give fair and efficient consideration to all uses, including those that are less well organized. How that should be done will vary from context to context, though there are far too many scenarios to list here. We shall address only a few of the possible adjustments that would bolster under-advocated uses. This chapter proposes restructuring a number of administrative management schemes to facilitate private transactions to allocate resources more efficiently and enhance environmental protection. These include, in addition to the Leshy-McUsic proposal on grazing, examples involving fisheries, water pollution, and agriculture. Other restructuring proposals would facilitate transactions between government entities to reallocate and improve the mix of resource uses; these would apply to the oceans and public lands.

Public management alone has not stopped the depletion of fisheries, as recounted in Chapter 1. An alternative is tradable catch permits. Under this approach—pioneered in New Zealand, Iceland, and Australia—the government sets a limit on the total allowable catch and then allocates individual tradable catch permits.[11] Who fishes and when is determined by a network of private actors with better information about weather, the condition of particular boats, and the price of fish than regulators could ever hope to gather and process intelligently. Regulations no longer force fishing fleets to risk their lives and boats in bad weather or to suffer artificially depressed prices because the entire year's catch landed in the same small time frame. Meanwhile, government still gets to limit the total annual catch and can also place some limits on the kind of equipment used.

This approach does not replace but instead restructures public management through the introduction of tradable permits. The design of the fisheries program parallels the cap-and-trade approach to pollution: government sets the goal, but a private network decides how to attain it. This new approach to fisheries has proved significantly more successful than hierarchical regulation at protecting fisheries, according to a systematic analysis of data from around the world.[12]

Although this approach has made some headway in the United States, Congress needs to remove some procedural obstacles it has erected to its wider use and otherwise promote its adoption. For example, 2006 congressional legislation authorized tradable permits in federal fisheries in New England and the Gulf of Mexico, but required the approval of participants in these fisheries in a referendum. This referendum requirement, which does not apply in other regional fisheries, creates an unnecessary additional hurdle in an already complex process for establishing tradable fisheries permits.[13]

Another opportunity for using network tools to improve public management and private transactions is water pollution control. In the thirty-eight years since the Clean Water Act was passed, there has been a major reduction in effluent from industrial facilities, municipal wastewater facilities, and other sources that discharge through pipes (called "point sources"). This progress has come primarily through direct federal regulations geared to what control technology is reasonably available for different categories of point sources. Nonetheless, many of the nation's waters remain polluted. Of the water bodies that have been assessed, 39 percent of river miles, 46 percent of lake acres, and 51 percent of estuarine areas fail to meet one or more water-quality standards.[14] A key reason is that, now that regulation has radically reduced water pollution from industry and municipalities, farmers have become a leading source of water pollution. For example, over "70 percent of the nitrogen and phosphorus delivered to the Gulf [of Mexico]," where there is a dead zone "larger than New Jersey," comes from agricultural nonpoint sources.[15] Improving the quality of these waters will require reducing pollution from farms and other sources whose discharge usually comes from runoff from the land ("nonpoint sources").

To reduce nonpoint pollution, it is necessary to make the Clean Water Act effective against agricultural sources. As the law professor Jonathan Cannon, a former EPA general counsel, argued at the "Breaking the Logjam" symposium, the most direct way of doing this is to require states to prepare and carry out implementation plans to achieve Total Maximum Daily Loads (TMDLs)—that is, the maximum daily loads of pollutants a water body can receive and still comply with water-quality standards. States are required to establish TMDLs for water bodies that do not satisfy water-quality standards even when technology-based standards are in place for point sources. In establishing a TMDL, states are also required to allocate total loadings between the point and nonpoint sources that affect the water body. This allocation creates an opportunity to engage nonpoint sources in reducing pollution. But this opportunity has often gone unrealized because EPA regulations do not require states to develop and carry out plans for implementing TMDLs.[16] As a result, there are no enforceable obligations on many nonpoint sources to reduce water pollution.

Getting states to adopt implementation plans that will impose pollution-reduction requirements on nonpoint sources will not be easy. The political obstacles are great. A classic example of a well-organized interest, farmers have considerable political power, both in Washington, D.C., and especially in states that emphasize agriculture. In fact the Clinton administration tried to require the preparation of implementation plans, but stiff opposition prompted the Bush administration to withdraw the requirement.[17]

There are also administrative complexities that stand in the way of requiring state implementation plans. Because changes in agricultural practices are generally the only way to reduce runoff from most farms, state plans would have to require changes in farming practices, and in sufficient detail to be enforceable. These specifications would have to vary widely according to what farms grow (pistachios or potatoes), how large the farm is (a few acres or many thousands), and how the land lies (sloped or flat, soil type), and many other factors. This complexity makes it difficult for a state plan to prescribe regulations that would achieve large reductions in nonpoint pollution, yet not be too vague to enforce or too ham-fisted to be acceptable politically. Vagueness in regulations could theoretically be cured through permits, but that would introduce the considerable risk of having national objectives be subverted at the local level. Experience under the Clean Air Act suggests that the federal government would have to specify minimum requirements for states to impose on farmers.[18] Writing regulations on farm practices at the national scale would be even more difficult than at the state level.

In sum, even if EPA had stronger legislative authority to push the states to regulate farms, it is unlikely that this, standing alone, would achieve needed reductions in water pollution from farms. For that reason, Cannon emphasizes that additional features are needed. To increase the likelihood that states will adopt effective implementation plans that impose appropriate obligations on nonpoint sources, Congress and the administration should reward agricultural operations that are subject to implementation plan requirements with easier access to the Department of Agriculture's farm-bill subsidies for conservation. Currently, the department spends more than $4 billion annually on conservation, a large share of it on general efforts for improving water quality, but these subsidies are generally not linked to local water quality problems.[19] These subsidies are potentially a powerful tool, but few efforts have been made to date to link them with the TMDL program. Linking these subsidies to water pollution control needs is an application of the crosscutting principle.

Market-based network regulation is another underused instrument for improving water quality that Cannon and others endorse. Under effluent trading, a source—say, a farmer—that reduces effluent more than legally required could get a water-pollution credit that could be sold to another source, which would then be permitted to discharge more than is otherwise legally allowed by a corresponding amount. This credit-trading system is a cousin of cap and trade for air pollution. EPA has tried to encourage effluent trading, but its potential has not been realized. One reason is that the statute forbids point sources from using credits from trades to meet effluent limitations of federal technology-based requirements. Also, the absence of binding obligations on nonpoint sources has limited farmers' interest in flexible instruments that would reduce pollution at lower cost. Further, trades need to be confined to sources whose effluent has a fungible impact on water quality. This means trades need to be confined to the same watershed, or even discrete portions of the same watershed, with the result that there may be few sources among which to trade. Within that limitation, the statute should be amended to explicitly authorize point sources to trade obligations to achieve technology-based standards.[20] Trading between point and nonpoint sources and among nonpoint sources should also be encouraged to the extent that it is possible to reliably estimate reductions in pollution from nonpoint sources.

Enabling point sources to pay farmers to reduce pollution would reduce farmers' opposition to inclusion in the water pollution control system. Moreover, such an approach would simplify administration because it would be the farmers rather than the EPA who choose many of the steps to reduce runoff.

Trading systems can also be used to enlist private resource managers in preventing climate change. As proposed in Chapter 5, supplementing cap and trade for greenhouse gases with a system of tradable credits for sources not covered by the cap would give forest owners, farmers, and others incentives to change their management practices to cut emissions or to absorb more carbon in trees or other vegetation. What's needed is a reliable means of measuring how much such changes in practices contribute to reducing greenhouse gases in the atmosphere and determining whether these practices are in fact changes from what would have been done anyway. The same problems arise in deciding the amount of effluent credits a farmer can sell for adopting farming practices that reduce pollution runoff. Analysts have worked on these problems, which can to some extent be addressed by using conservative default values in calculating the amount of credits, but there is more work to be done to make the methodologies reliable for mass application.[21] The stakes are too high not to be careful, but the efficiencies from trading are so great, and so necessary to win support for stronger environmental protection, that solving the methodological challenges must be a priority.

These various trading schemes could become even more powerful when used in combination. For example, a farmer who turns crop land abutting a stream into woods not only sequesters carbon but also reduces runoff of fertilizer and pesticides that add to water pollution, protects against floods, and improves the quality of drinking water. Even more benefit may ensue if the woods contain wetlands. To emphasize that these benefits have economic as well as environmental dimensions, analysts sometimes call them "ecosystem services." If government succeeds in finding reliable ways to measure ecosystem services in the form of stored carbon and water pollution avoided, as it can do if it broadens its horizons beyond hierarchical regulation, the learning should spread to measuring other ecosystem services. When that happens, a landowner can get multiple economic rewards for taking a single action with multiple environmental benefits.[22] The economic and environmental rewards would come through marketplace transactions, but it will be a market for environmental protection, constructed and overseen by government. This is an application of the principles in favor of new tools and crosscutting approaches.

Another environmental problem requiring different forms of structural reform in current laws is the government's management of ocean resources. Some federal statutes regulating marine resources, such as the Magnuson-Stevens Act, give federal agencies very broad discretion to manage resources for multiple purposes, on the premise that the agencies can be trusted to choose the best use of a given resource in a given location without meaningful guidance from Congress. All too often, however, well-organized interests—as in the grazing problem —exercise undue influence over agency decisions, resulting in environmental degradation and other misallocations.

A solution is to shift the locus of decision from the agencies to Congress through a system of statutory zoning of ocean uses. The federal government controls the portions of the oceans that lie between three and two hundred miles off our shores. This "Exclusive Economic Zone," larger than the land area of the United States, is an environmental treasure and potentially an economic one as well. The government, however, has been a poor steward, as illustrated by its allowing overfishing. Most major U.S. fisheries, in both federal and state waters, are governed by regional management bodies in which environmental interests have little voice. These bodies are dominated by commercial fishery interests that generally take a very short-term view and constantly seek higher catch levels, even though these lead to overfishing and are not sustainable.

Someone who knows that from experience is Josh Eagle, a law professor and participant in the "Breaking the Logjam" project. In his prior capacity as an attorney for the National Audubon Society, Eagle served in the late 1990s as a representative on a panel that provided recommendations to the Atlantic States Marine Fisheries Commission on various management issues related to crab and eel fisheries. The commission usually took the panel's advice. Unfortunately, from Eagle's perspective, he was the only environmental advocate on the advisory panel, with the result that he was routinely outvoted. He came to the conclusion that the environmental protection interests he represented would be better served if they controlled one-eighteenth of the region instead of one losing vote out of eighteen.[23]

Eagle and his coauthors urge that Congress itself allocate various portions of the federally controlled portion of the ocean to different uses, such as nature preservation, commercial fishing, recreational fishing, oil and gas drilling, renewable energy, and so on.[24] These zones would continue to be controlled by the federal government, but their management would be divided among various federal agencies according to their area of specialization. Zoning, by facing trade-offs in a process that looks at the ocean comprehensively and separates conflicting uses, can advance a variety of goals. They include not only preserving parts of the ocean in their natural state and protecting fish stocks but also allowing more offshore oil and gas drilling in appropriate places, as well as setting aside spaces for renewable sources of energy such as wind farms and tidal energy.

Nature preservation and recreational uses would fare better, Eagle believes, if Congress made the basic choices through a high-visibility decision on zoning rather than by burying the choices in a low-visibility administrative process.[25] This is an application of the principle in favor of more openness on trade-offs.

Once the zones are established, their presumptive assignment to a particular use would narrow the range of interests competing to use each zone. That could help interests that are not well organized and are therefore at a comparative disadvantage in acting collectively. In zones dedicated to preservation, for example, interests that favor it would not be up against better-organized interests that favor exploitative uses.[26]

As a second part of the solution, the initial allocation of uses among zones could be only presumptive, subject to reallocation through interest group/agency bargaining.[27] So, for example, the agency charged with managing an ocean segment zoned for preservation and conservation groups allied with that agency might agree to allow some commercial fishing in return for, say, the agency in charge of an ocean segment zoned for commercial fishing and its fisherfolk allies taking extra steps helpful to preservation. The outcome would be that a network of agencies would share the work of managing the federally controlled portions of the ocean, informed by the knowledge and preferences of their respective constituencies. A form of bargaining among agencies and their interest group allies could produce superior resource allocations in a flexible process analogous to the market-based solutions discussed earlier in this chapter. Environmental and preservation interests would fare better than under the traditional multiple use system of hierarchical management because the congressional legislation, made through open political processes, would give environment-oriented agencies an initial entitlement to manage portions of the oceans zoned for conservation, giving them and their environmental group allies significant leverage in subsequent bargaining.

Similar in many ways to zoning the ocean is a proposal to straighten out the scattershot pattern of federal land ownership, especially in the west. The federal government owns approximately 28 percent of the land area of the United States, including almost 50 percent of the land in eleven western states and about two-thirds of the land in Alaska.[28] Unfortunately, federal holdings in many places are neither contiguous nor along lines that make environmental or economic sense today. To the contrary, owing to various accidents of history, they are sometimes as scattered as the squares on a checkerboard—indeed, in some instances laid out precisely in a checkerboard pattern bearing no correspondence to ecosystem boundaries.

This random pattern of federal land holdings causes many problems. Federal land agencies cannot properly manage environmentally sensitive areas because they are intermixed with private or state-owned lands. States and localities cannot properly plan and develop urban communities because they have grown up around federally owned parcels.

The sensible solution is evident in the abstract: trades in which the federal government exchanges land it does not need it for land it does. There are statutes that do allow for such swaps, but they are too cumbersome to make any substantial dent in the irrational pattern of federal land ownership. As a result, Congress itself must legislate on such minor matters as conferring 1.5 acres to a county for a fire-fighting facility or clarifying title to a cemetery that a county has operated since before the Forest Service was founded.[29]

Senate Majority Leader Harry Reid and his fellow senator from Nevada, John Ensign, have, however, found a way around the administrative thicket. They instituted an intergovernmental trading process in which the state and local governments concerned with the area around Las Vegas, together with environmental, business, and civic groups, negotiated a comprehensive program that in cluded auctioning some federal lands and using some of the proceeds for the federal government to purchase additional lands in environmentally sensitive areas. The deal also called for wilderness designations of some federal lands, both newly acquired and old. The negotiated package was then put in a bill, which promptly passed Congress and was signed into law. Building on that success, two additional programs were negotiated for other areas in Nevada and enacted into law.[30]

The issue is how to replicate this success in trading resource uses in other places and to make the reallocations of uses more responsive to expert assessments and less responsive to the vagaries of congressional politics. The next chapter suggests a mechanism to do so: expert panels that would gather information, talk to the interest groups, and propose a balanced solution for congressional action.

This chapter has addressed a limited but varied and important subset of natural resource issues. Its specific recommendations are designed to bring fairer consideration of less well organized interests, especially preservation and conservation interests. The ultimate point is, however, that similar reforms are needed for similar natural resource problems.

Recommendations on Natural Resources

Land

Authorize tradable credits for greenhouse gas reductions in agriculture and forestry:

- As part of climate legislation establishing a cap-and-trade system for greenhouse gases, Congress should authorize issuance of credits to farmers and forestry enterprises that voluntarily adopt resource management measures to reduce their emissions or sequester additional carbon. These credits could be sold to sources subject to cap-and-trade as offsets to their emissions.

Allow grazing permits to be permanently retired:

- Congress should authorize and require the Bureau of Land Management and the U.S. Forest Service to permanently retire federal land from grazing if the holder of a grazing permit requests the withdrawal. This would allow ranchers to sell their grazing permits voluntarily to buyers, such as conservationists, who are willing to pay for the permits in order to restore the ecological health of federal lands.

Rationalize scattershot pattern of federal land ownership:

- Congress should create a commission to propose changes in federal land holdings to make them more contiguous and effective in achieving their environmental and other purposes.

Water

Use economic incentives to reduce water pollution from nonpoint sources:

- The administration should require states to develop implementation plans, based on Total Maximum Daily Loads for achieving ambient water-quality standards, that specify regulatory obligations for point and nonpoint sources. If legally necessary, Congress should amend the Clean Water Act to require states to develop these implementation plans.

- The administration should reward agricultural sources covered by state implementation plans with greater ease of access to United States Department of Agriculture farm-bill subsidy programs.

- To encourage point sources to participate in effluent trading, Congress should amend the statute to allow point sources greater latitude to trade obligations to achieve technology-based standards, provided the trading would not result in pollution hot spots.

Oceans

Start the process of zoning U.S. oceans:

- Working with the administration, Congress should pass legislation creating an Oceans Zoning Commission. The commission should be charged with developing legislation, within one or two years, for zoning federal ocean waters in the U.S. Exclusive Economic Zone, which are generally the waters between three and two hundred nautical miles from the shore.

- The commission should be made up of experts who can take the broad view in formulating a process for zoning the oceans. The Commission should consult with, but not delegate decisionmaking to, marine stakeholders such as federal agencies, coastal states and cities, conservationists, oil and gas, renewable energy, fishing, aquaculture, shipping, navigation, and mining interests.

- Among the issues the commission should be called upon to address in crafting legislation that would enable ocean zoning are: what institution should zone the oceans; what Congress's role should be in ocean zoning; what criteria should be used in establishing zones; whether certain areas of the oceans should be zoned before others; and how the zones should be managed after they are established. In addressing these issues, the commission should draw on experiences with municipal zoning and the federal government's experience managing federally owned public lands.

Promote use of tradable fishing quotas in wild fisheries:

- To help rebuild depleted wild fish stocks, the administration should introduce more programs to limit fish catches by distributing tradable fishing quotas to fishermen. Congress should facilitate the spread of such programs in fisheries by removing several impediments to their initiation in the Magnuson-Stevens Fishery Conservation and Management Reauthorization Act of 2006.

These recommendations accord with our four principles:

Principle 1: New regulatory tools as complements for traditional hierarchical regulation. The recommendations on grazing, fishing, water pollution, greenhouse gases, and ecosystem services introduce elements of marketplace transactions or property-like rights into public management schemes. The recommendations on zoning the oceans and rationalizing federal land ownership patterns introduce trading between public entities.

Principle 2: Realignment of federal and state responsibilities. The proposal on federal lands would realign ownership patterns to broaden federal control over areas of federal interest and, concomitantly, give states and localities more independence over other areas.

Principle 3: Trade-offs faced openly on the basis of reliable information. The proposal on grazing would raise to high visibility a fundamental issue, whether to allow holders of permits to retire them via a market mechanism, most likely to bring retirements where the trade-offs between ranching and the impacts of grazing most favor retirement. The proposal on water pollution would begin the process of facing the trade-offs on agricultural runoff. The proposal on sequestration of carbon would be subservient to the cap-and-trade program on greenhouse gases, where the trade-offs are made in setting the cap. Zoning the oceans would force high visibility decisions on allocating the ocean to various uses.

Principle 4: Crosscutting regulatory approaches. The proposal to subsidize farmers to take a variety of environmentally beneficial actions, from reducing greenhouse gases to protecting wetlands, illustrates this principle. So does the proposal to zone the oceans and then reallocate uses through trading, and the proposal for land swaps.

CHAPTER 7

Smarter Government
The Tool-Wielding Monkey

The best addition to brownies or turkey stuffing is the rich, strongly flavored kernel of the black walnut tree. The nuts must be gathered after they ripen (but before other creatures make off with them), husked, dried for several weeks in a cool, secure place, and then cracked open. Some people do the husking by driving over the nuts with their cars, the drying by stowing them in their attic, and the cracking by blows from a hammer.

Black walnut (*Juglans nigra*) in the husk, in the shell, and cracked open.
© 2009 D. Paulus-Jagrič.

A capuchin monkey (*Cebus libidinosus*) wielding a stone tool. Courtesy of Elisabetta Visalberghi and the EthoCebus Project.

Getting to the kernel of the palm nut is also tough, but the capuchin monkeys of Boa Vista, Brazil, can do it, even though they lack cars, attics, and steel hammers. The monkeys tap the nuts to determine ripeness, remove the husk, bite off the tip of the shell (the only part that they can pierce with their teeth), drink the liquid inside, and set the shells aside to dry for several days, which makes them easier to crack. To crack the nuts, the monkeys devise their own sort of hammer: heavy rocks that they haul to the work site. In selecting rocks, they reject those likely to crack or crumble in use.[1]

The environmental policy nut to be cracked is reconciling environmental quality with prosperity. New regulatory tools will help. We have described them in the three previous chapters. But cracking that nut also requires facing trade-offs openly, having reliable information, tapping expert ideas, and taking account of the crosscutting nature of environmental problems. These require-ments are particularly tough because of the complexity of environ-mental issues, the polarization of environmental politics, the com-partmentalization of environmental agencies and congressional committees, and the separate roles of Congress and executive agen-cies. The new regulatory tools will help with this part of the chal-lenge too, but we also need new decisionmaking methods, the sub-ject of this chapter. If, like the monkeys, we arrange to use the right tools, we can crack the nut.

Helping Congress Update Environmental Statutes

In federal environmental statutes, Congress has generally opted to leave even the most central questions about trade-offs to agencies. By telling agencies to manage land for multiple uses, natural re-source statutes have the agencies arbitrate between competing uses. By telling EPA to reduce risk or reduce emissions without giving meaningful instructions on how much, the pollution stat-utes have the agency strike the balance between the benefits of controlling pollution and the costs of doing so.[2]

Leaving the most important trade-offs to agencies is an inevi-table consequence of the statutes' requiring use of traditional hier-archical regulatory tools. Such tools often require someone to issue a huge number of directives—in the case of air pollution, directives to many tens of thousands of sources. Congress lacks the capacity to hand down all these individuated orders, and there is no evident means for it to give precise directions to the agency on how to do so.

The network tools recommended in previous chapters would, in contrast, both allow and encourage Congress to face more of the key trade-offs itself. Consider the acid rain program, for example. In deciding how low to set the cap, Congress dealt with the trade-off between reducing acid rain and increasing compliance costs, effec-tively deciding the level of effort it required from industry. In dis-tributing the allowances, Congress allocated burdens among power plants and, through them, among electricity consumers. Even though Congress could not make these pivotal choices when the regulatory system was hierarchical, it can do so with cap and trade because it vastly simplifies the decisions that government needs to make. It is the network rather than government that decides which sources would do what to stay within the cap. Thus, the big trade-offs are made in the most visible way—crystallized by Congress in a statute.[3]

Congress could in theory leave pivotal decisions such as the level of a cap or the allocation of allowances to the agency, but there are political reasons why Congress would tend not to do so, as exemplified in the case of acid rain. With the large economic and environmental stakes apparent to many voters, Congress could not leave setting the cap and the method of allocating the allowances to EPA anymore than it could let the Internal Revenue Service set the income tax rates. Moreover, unless legislators pin down these high-visibility choices, their opponents in the next election could portray the likely outcome of the agency's deliberations in terms most unfavorable to the incumbents. So, with network approaches, not only could Congress make the pivotal choices, but politics would prompt it to do so.

Having Congress face the key trade-offs itself rather than leaving them to agencies brings key advantages. Agencies tend to be lower-visibility forums, where less organized interests have even less purchase, as illustrated by the overgrazing and ocean examples already discussed. In other cases, agencies seek to duck the hard choices Congress has left them. EPA has sometimes reacted to Congress's handing off a controversial choice by postponing a decision with the result that the public must wait years for protection. For example, the 1970 Clean Air Act told EPA to regulate especially hazardous air pollutants to eliminate any harm to health, although this would require costs that would have been staggering. To avoid confronting the trade-offs, EPA, with only a few exceptions, failed for twenty years to set any hazardous air standards.[4]

Moreover, when it leaves basic choices to agencies, Congress frames the statute to require the agency to follow such-and-such procedures and consider such-and-such factors. These requirements seldom limit the agency's range of choice, but they delay the choice and create snares that may invalidate agency action on judicial review.[5] Meanwhile, members of Congress attempt to influence how the agency exercises the broad discretion that Congress has assigned it.

Agencies try to survive judicial review and deflect the political pressure on controversial choices by pretending, in what has been called a "science charade," that science dictated the chosen results. But science hardly ever does so specifically. For example, EPA set particulate matter standards that failed to protect against major risks, and simultaneously set ozone standards that protect against far less serious risks; EPA invoked science to justify a politically opportune difference in outcomes.[6]

The harm to science can be even more blatant. Political appointees at agencies sometimes lean on career scientists to make the science support the politically convenient outcome. For instance, a report by the Inspector General at the Department of Interior found thirteen occasions on which an appointed official pressured scientists to make certain findings in order to avoid having to take steps to protect endangered species.[7]

An additional victim is open government. EPA, for example, is required to adopt thousands of detailed regulations for different pollutants, wastes, and sources on the basis of highly complex, though in the end indecisive, statutory instructions. The esoteric details in all the regulations and intermediate determinations underlying them obscure the basic trade-offs and make it extremely difficult for the public to understand them. As a result, democratic debate and government accountability for important decisions are badly undermined.

To base its decision on reliable information, Congress needs to select the right tools, just like the monkey, because the information necessary to make environmental trade-offs is far from simple. To set the cap for a cap-and-trade program, for example, requires the input of many kinds of experts. Physicians, epidemiologists, and toxicologists are needed to define, say, the impact of a pollutant on the human body: atmospheric scientists explain how that pollutant moves in the atmosphere, engineers treat the feasibility of controlling its emissions, and economists establish costs. Their expertise will not, however, dictate the decision, because the technical findings and the trade-offs among them are usually subject to a large range of uncertainty, and balancing competing considerations depends on human values rather than on scientific findings. To bridge the gap between values and science, and to tee up the question for decision, Congress needs help, especially because it has so many pressing responsibilities and can deal with only so many topics. As Phil Sharp, a former Congressman and the president of Resources for the Future, put it at the project's symposium, Congress has only a limited capacity ("bandwidth" was the word he used) to process information.[8]

Another symposium participant, E. Donald Elliott, formerly an EPA general counsel and now head of the worldwide environmental law department of a major law firm as well as a Yale Law School professor, agrees with Sharp, but suggests a solution. "Most environmental problems are too complex and nuanced to be addressed effectively by a politicized and generalist Congress. The function of Congress is not to devise solutions to complex technocratic problems, but to provide democratic legitimacy." His prescription is for Congress or the administration to "build an ancillary institution with the time and expertise to hammer out policy changes and present them to the Congress for ratification."[9]

Elliott marshals abundant precedent for his prescription. Congress has successfully used expert bodies to propose solutions for congressional ratification in many contexts, including framing court rules and closing unneeded military bases. States use law revision commissions to propose reforms to their legislatures. The

European Union deals with environmental issues by the experts at the European Commission proposing new legislation to the European Council and Parliament. Elliott ruefully concludes, "The United States Congress stands out internationally as one of the few places where the task of developing and proposing legislation on complex technical subjects is left to the legislators."[10]

Congress could launch an expert proposal system in one of two ways. It could task an existing agency, such as EPA, to construct the proposal, or it could create a special-purpose expert commission to deal with a particular environmental problem. One advantage of a special commission, Elliott argues, is that it could be like the panels of the National Academy of Sciences, whose members, if not uniformly disinterested, at least agree to disclose and put aside their biases rather than lobby on behalf of a particular institutional concern, such as an industry, an environmental group, or the agency itself.[11] A commission constituted in this way is particularly likely to propose win-win solutions.

The mandate of Congress to an expert proposal system should not only specify the problem to be addressed (e.g., climate change and air pollution) and the legal structure to deal with it (e.g., an integrated market-based approach as detailed in Chapters 4 and 5), but also tell the commission to propose the substantive rules (e.g., numeric caps on emissions of particular pollutants and how to distribute allowances.) Under a cap-and-trade regime, the caps should be designed so that savings from network solutions are shared between advancing environmental protection further than would have been achieved through traditional hierarchical regulation and lowering what would otherwise be the costs of compliance. A similar approach should be followed in the case of natural resource management and other environmental programs. Such a win-win outcome is essential for ultimate passage. Finally, the agency or commission should translate the results into statutory language.

In legislation soliciting a proposal from an agency or commission, Congress could establish an expedited schedule for legislative consideration of the resulting proposal. It might go even further, restricting its options to accepting or rejecting the recommendations, as it did with the Defense Base Realignment Closure Commission.[12] There are many options, and different ones may be appropriate for different environmental problems.

Should Congress fail to launch expert proposal systems, the president could task an agency to make proposals or appoint a commission to do so. In addition, a sufficiently diverse group of outside experts can also at least start the process of proposing legislation on their own initiative. The "Breaking the Logjam" project has sought to do just that for a wide range of environmental problems.

Even if Congress takes on many of the key choices, it will still inevitably leave decisions to agencies. In so doing, Congress should enhance their ability to face trade-offs openly and using reliable information by equipping them with tools to (1) assess the results of expert studies, (2) systematically array alternatives and the considerations involved in choosing among them, and (3) get feedback from informed individuals.

Improving Agency Decision Making

An agency assessment of expert studies is plagued not only by the tendency to conflate science with politics and the agency's own policy preferences (the science charade) but also by the sharply adversarial terms in which stakeholders pose the scientific findings to agency staff and the underfunding of agency science. As Donald Elliott put it, "The decline of science as an important determinant in environmental decision making is in many ways the underlying subtext of Justice Stephen Breyer's book, *Breaking the Vicious Circle: Toward Effective Risk Regulation.* In case after case, the book shows how decision making, particularly in the environmental area, has become political and science has been precluded from playing its rightful role. . . . Science is being increasingly marginalized and is playing less of a role in the decision-making process, particularly at my old agency, EPA."[13]

Judicial review is insufficient to cure these problems in that it begins only after the agency has made its decision, and it is a blunt instrument. Judges rarely flunk the agency decisions for questionable science unless the errors are gross and palpable, even to non-scientist judges. Much bad agency science passes this forgiving standard, but in the cases that it does flunk, the consequences can be dire. The rule must go back to the agency for years of additional work and new judicial review. Meanwhile, in many cases, the rule cannot be enforced.[14]

Somewhat more responsive to the problems plaguing agency science are the groups of outside scientists that the statutes require EPA to assemble to assess its scientific or technical assessments.[15] They include a Science Advisory Board and a Clean Air Scientific Advisory Committee. EPA typically sends such groups agency science assessments only after years of in-house work. At this late date, it may be difficult to correct fundamental problems without causing long delays. These advisory groups are helpful, but their mandate is too limited and their review comes too late.

Two "Breaking the Logjam" project participants, Angus Macbeth and Gary Marchant, have diagnosed problems with EPA science and suggested a way to improve the process by giving outside advisory groups a broader mandate.[16] Macbeth's career spans litigating for the Natural Resources Defense Council, serving as deputy assistant attorney general under President Jimmy Carter, and heading the environmental practice of a major law firm. Marchant holds a science doctorate, was a partner at a major law firm, and now is a professor and head of a law-science institute.

Macbeth and Marchant's proposal would move EPA science assessment in the direction of the Health Effects Institute that EPA helped launch in 1980. It is a private nonprofit body dedicated to developing scientific understanding of the health effects of toxic pollutants from motor vehicles and other products. The institute has a board of directors that has stood for independence and expertise. Its funding comes from both the EPA and industry.[17] The institute identifies issues in need of scientific research, commissions studies by universities and research organizations through open competitive processes, and evaluates the results of these studies and others in a nonadversarial way. Rather than reviewing particular regulatory decisions, the institute seeks to identify and commissions research to help resolve the most important scientific uncertainties relevant to future regulatory policies.

Macbeth and Marchant propose that Congress require EPA to work with a group of outside scientists whose function would be much broader, and start earlier, than that of the current Science Advisory Board and Clean Air Scientific Advisory Board. In particular, EPA should be required to consult this group early in the agency process of assessing the science and developing regulatory options for addressing an environmental problem. Earlier consultation is essential. Most science and engineering work at EPA is not original research conducted by agency personnel but rather analysis of studies done elsewhere. The advisory group, if involved early, could steer the agency toward commissioning additional original research where there are critical gaps in the data and help the agency design the best methods of analysis from the outset. It should also promote consideration of alternative regulatory tools. This is a more constructive role than weighing the adequacy of information after the analysis is done and regulations drafted.

The advisory group would also be tasked with trying to get agency scientists and their counterparts from academic and research institutions, regulated industries, and environmental groups to agree at the outset on how the science or engineering assessment should be done. Such agreement could speed the assessment and head off litigation over the agency science. Whether full consensus is achieved, the effort may temper the adversarial nature of the current process. To encourage participation by all sides, the advisory group should have funds to subsidize participation by scientists representing environmental and local community groups.

Congress should build analogous advisory systems into other environmental agencies.

Improving Agency Decision Making: Cost-Benefit Analysis

A sound assessment of the information provided by various technical specialties helps predict the consequences of the actions being considered, but it does not dictate a decision. A number of alternatives (including no action) should be considered, and different considerations will weigh for or against different alternatives. A systematic analysis of various considerations is useful in making a sound regulatory decision, whether the decisionmaker is Congress or an agency. Not only should such an analysis put the pros and cons into sharper relief, but it also should bring to light more innovative alternatives that produce more "pro" for less "con."[18] Such a regulatory impact analysis should be included when an expert commission or agency proposes legislation to Congress, as is already the case when an agency proposes or promulgates a regulation. The analysis is, of course, only a tool, and the decision ultimately must be made by humans exercising judgment, but good tools help people do better work.

Administrations under presidents of both parties have done regulatory impact studies through cost-benefit analysis of the trade-offs involved in different ways of implementing the statutes. Regulatory impact analysis overtly weighs pros and cons, often by valuing them in terms of dollars. The methodology is, in brief, to (1) identify the proposed action, often a new regulation, (2) identify alternatives to it, (3) identify the most important impacts of the action and the alternatives, (4) quantify those impacts, (5) value the impacts in dollar terms to the extent possible, and (6) compare the total (and, under the better practice, incremental) costs and benefits of the proposed action and the alternatives.

Issues arise at each step. To illustrate, in the case of a proposed rule to reduce a pollutant, the impacts to be identified might include better health from reduced pollution and the costs of installing pollution-control equipment to achieve the reduction. That much is obvious. But a rule to reduce that one pollutant might incidentally reduce others. Should the analysis consider this collateral benefit? There also might be collateral costs. For example, a rule banning one chemical may increase use of another chemical with its own risks. Such collateral impacts must be considered even-handedly.[19]

Particularly serious problems arise at the fifth step—valuing the impacts in monetary terms. It is relatively straightforward to the extent the impacts involve the purchase of goods and services available in the marketplace, such as the cost of building a hydroelectric dam or revenue from selling the electricity it produces. Valuing impacts becomes more difficult the more remote they are from marketplace activity. Another consequence of the dam might be imperiling an endangered species. Also difficult to value are actions whose consequences include impacts on human health. The consequence of a rule to reduce air pollution might be to decrease predicted overall deaths from 30,008 to 30,006 out of 1,000,000 people, among a population of 300,000,000. If the prediction is accurate, the rule would save 600 statistical lives. Some analysts would impute a monetary value for a statistical life saved by considering factors such as the wage differential between otherwise similar jobs that carry differing risks of death from occupational causes or how much people voluntarily pay to lower risks, for example, by buying safer cars or enhanced health care. For them, the value of the benefit would then be the price of a statistical life multiplied by 600. Other analysts would not put a monetary value on lives saved.[20]

The final step, to compare the costs and benefits of the alternatives, is simple in the sense that it only requires adding up the relevant costs and benefits and comparing them. But uncertainties in estimating consequences and other uncertainties in putting a price on them generate a range of costs and of benefits for each alternative, complicating the comparison. Another problem is whether and how to discount to net present value costs and benefits that will occur in the future. In making investment decisions, both businesses and governments generally discount future economic benefits, such as the electricity produced in the future from a dam constructed with costs incurred this year, on the premise that benefits enjoyed today are worth more to individuals and society than future benefits. But should this logic be applied to health benefits of environmental regulation, such as the cancers that would otherwise occur twenty-five years from now that are prevented by incurring costs today to reduce pollution exposures, and if so, what should the discount rate be? These questions are highly controversial. Also, a comparison of the totals of costs and benefits tells us nothing about whether the costs and benefits are fairly distributed. Nor can it readily take into account important qualities of these two factors. In most cost-benefit analysis, for example, a death is a death, but it may make a great deal of difference to people whether a death is by cancer or an accident. There are methods to deal with some of these problems, but they increase complexity and bring with them more value judgments.

Further, some scholars object to cost-benefit analysis on the basis that it is inappropriate to place a price on such "priceless" things as human life. Others, some who surely cannot be dismissed as pro-industry apologists, favor its use, at least as a source of information for considerations along with other factors rather than a cut-and-dried formula for decisionmaking.[21] Individuals implicitly weigh life versus costs when, for example, they decide what premium to pay for a safer car, but it is quite another matter for government to place a price tag on individual lives in deciding, for example, whether reducing risks from pollution is worth the cost. Yet, government does weigh life against cost when it decides whether to take extra measures to reduce highway fatalities or avert murders. Government must weigh life against cost in the pollution-control field because the cost for eliminating environmental risk altogether is infinite.

The choice is therefore not whether to weigh lives saved against cost but how to do so. At a minimum, government needs to be open about trade-offs, but that does not necessarily require placing a dollar value on a statistical life. The analysis might weigh some pros and cons at their market prices and weigh other impacts, such as risk to human life, in other metrics, such as statistical lives saved. In either event, it would still be up to the decisionmaker to come to the final decision, using cost-benefit analysis as only one input. Regardless of the precise method used, the regulatory impact analysis is not the decisionmaker in itself but merely a tool to be used by the person making the decision. Nonetheless, such analysis can make enormously beneficial contributions by disciplining the decision process, systematically examining alternatives, looking closely at all the major consequences, generating information on trade-offs, and structuring evaluation of options. Such an approach stands in stark contrast to how National Ambient Air Quality Standards are set under the Clean Air Act, where the statute requires EPA to deny that it engages in such trade-offs even though they are inevitable.[22] This is not open government.

A further issue is that, under the current system, the Office of Information and Regulatory Affairs in the Office of Management and Budget reviews proposals by agencies to adopt major new regulations and the accompanying regulatory analyses but does not have any systematic process for reviewing agencies' failure to adopt new regulations, even though their environmental and other benefits substantially exceed their costs.[23] This asymmetry in the process may introduce an antiregulatory bias. Devising a workable process to require agencies to conduct a cost-benefit analysis regarding a lack of agency regulation is difficult, but the task should be pursued.

The president needs to take responsibility for coming up with a protocol for regulatory impact analysis that is even-handed and open. This job is important because regulatory impact analysis affects every area of environmental protection. The Office of Information and Regulatory Affairs now provides a protocol, but some scholars and advocates argue that the methodology that the federal environmental agencies now use exaggerates regulatory costs and underestimates regulatory benefits, while others argue the opposite. To break the adversarial gridlock, the president should task an expert commission to propose guidelines for regulatory impact analysis in environmental decisions. To its credit, the Obama administration has launched a review of the existing Executive Order.[24]

Improving Agency Decision Making: Listening to a Broader Range of Experts

Dan Esty's observation that regulatory tools should be designed so that it is not just "a few thousand smart folks" in an agency but "millions of smart people" who come up with innovations applies also to the method by which government makes environmental decisions.[25] Agencies and special commissions should not be the only ones that propose or evaluate new regulatory measures. This work also should be informed by a broad range of experts from outside government.

The process that the federal government now uses to solicit public participation in regulatory decisionmaking falls far short of getting the help reasonably available from a broad range of experts in academia, medicine, engineering, industry, state and local government, and elsewhere. Congress, in the 1946 Administrative Procedure Act, did require agencies to invite comments from the public on their rules.[26] An agency must solicit comments on a proposed rule through the *Federal Register,* a daily publication that with its three columns of fine print on each of its hundreds of pages resembles a phone book. Each week government agencies propose dozens of new regulations. Apart from libraries, the *Federal Register* is circulated to and read chiefly by officials, lawyers, lobbyists, and advocacy groups. At the beginning of the modern environmental era in the early 1970s, the comments on proposed environmental rules came mostly from big corporations, big unions, state agencies, and trade associations. Later, as national environmental groups grew and became better organized and funded, they commented more frequently, and on some rules their comments began to rival those of businesses in sophistication.

The upshot, however, has been that just about the only experts who participate in the comments are those who work on behalf of an agency, industry, or advocacy groups. They, however, often constitute only a narrow slice of the experts with relevant expertise. Most experts never know of the rulemaking.

This did not change when agencies began to post their proposed rules on the Internet, invited comments to be submitted on the site, and posted those comments for comment. (Some commentators prevent rebuttal to their contentions by hand-submitting their comments at the last minute.) These bows to the Internet do little to change the workings of the system as it was established in 1946, when the stamp for mailing a first-class letter cost three cents. It is the rare individual, other than someone who works with a stakeholder organization, who knows of these proposed regulations, let alone reads them or understands the contested points of information upon which the final decision rests. Environmental organizations do use the Internet to urge members to submit comments, sometimes generating half a million short emails, short letters, or postcards on a single rule, but these comments generally express a generalized preference for stronger regulation rather than providing pointed information. Instead of reading public comments, some agencies send most of them to contractors who compile them.[27] That is how irrelevant they are to the actual decision.

The federal government should use the Internet to get input from knowledgeable individuals that increases the relevance and reliability of information used in its environmental decisions and generates ideas for smarter alternatives.[28] This requires two steps. First, agencies should augment their formulaic requests for comments on the proposed rule with separately stated requests for comments on specific points of information important to the definition of the problem, the range of possible solutions, and their consequences. Second, the agency should set up a process that sorts and posts comments by the specific points discussed and enables individual experts to evaluate, rank, and annotate one another's contentions through a Wiki process of interactive network collaboration. This can be done through online tools commonly used in consumer Web applications. Experts can use these and other Internet forums to discuss and debate the issues, and to submit their views to the agency. These processes would increase the reliability of submitted information and decrease the workload of policymakers.

Professor Beth Noveck, one of the originators of this proposal on the use of the Internet and a project participant who now is United States Deputy Chief Technology Officer for Open Government in the Executive Office of the President, has already shown how this can be done in the patent context. The United States Patent Office is now trying out her system on some categories of patent applications, as are the UK Patent Office, the European Patent Office, and the Japan Patent Office.[29] The Patent Office gets a good sense of the opinion of the informed expertise in the field but still decides whether to grant the patent.

By opening a "suggestion box," the agency can bring in a much broader range of scientists, engineers, physicians, economists, ecologists, or other experts. Those with specialized knowledge could understand its relevance without having to plow through the dozens or even hundreds of pages that constitute the notice of the rulemaking in the *Federal Register*. Instead, communities of experts will learn via specialized blogs, chat rooms, Internet newsletters, email distribution lists, and the like that their knowledge can shed light on an important public policy question. These experts will include academics, staffs of research institutions, physicians, consulting engineers, and employees of industry, nonprofits, governments. Of particular interest when a specific industry is being regulated will be those who have retired from that industry and so are freer to speak their minds. In general, instead of the organized interest groups with a vested economic or other policy stake in the rulemaking outcome having de facto control over which experts will participate, a much broader range of experts could self-select themselves as participants.

The current commenting process is not conducive to a conversation among experts. Individual scientists do not have the resources to sort through prior comments to find what was said on the aspect they know about. What we have instead is a process in which individuals and organizations talk at government rather than to one another. It is at heart a hierarchical system. By organizing the process so that commentators could communicate and evaluate one another's comments by topic, agencies would facilitate participation by communities of knowledgeable individuals. Were some organizations to still withhold their comments until the last minute, they would run the risk that expert opinion would coalesce against them before they weighed in.

This format for commenting could be used in many contexts. It is applicable whether the proposal being developed is for action by Congress or an agency. The science advisory group system recommended above could use it early in the assessment process to vet thoughts on how to help structure the agency's analysis of scientific issues and regulatory options. Expert commissions could use it in developing proposals to zone the oceans or realign federal land holdings.[30]

Addressing Crosscutting Environmental Problems

The work of almost all federal departments and agencies impacts the environment in some way. Even if the environmental dimension of these agencies' work could be severed from the other dimensions and all put in one department, environmental protection would still be compartmentalized for the same reason that the EPA itself is now compartmentalized: given the number of issues and the size and diversity of the country, division of labor in collecting and analyzing information and making decisions is inevitable. The problem of decisionmaking fragmentation exists in the legislative branch too, where a surprisingly large number of committees and subcommittees have a say in environmental issues. For example, climate change legislation gets attention from committees and subcommittees concerned with not only environment, energy, and natural resources but also commerce, finance, appropriations, and more. The compartmentalization in the executive branch and the legislative branch is compounded because, given the separation of powers ordained in the Constitution, both have a say and the legislative branch is also divided.

We therefore concentrate here on institutional changes that would help the federal government deal with crosscutting problems. Some of the proposals made so far will help. Using separate hierarchical regulations to address crosscutting problems such as climate change and criteria air pollutants would create serious clashes. But properly designed network approaches can complement each other, as climate change and criteria air pollutants again exemplify. This, however, takes us only part of the way to vindicating the principle. Additional changes are necessary so that government can see the environmental-protection forest for the trees.

Congress should require an annual report on the state of the environment, with special reference to crosscutting issues. The Council on Environmental Quality in the Executive Office of the President did at one point prepare quite substantial State of the Environment reports, but the practice has been abandoned. It is worth noting that in the European Commission's Environment Directorate-General performs Annual Environment Policy Reviews that consider the entire range of environmental issues.[31]

There is little likelihood that Congress will rationalize the jurisdiction of its committees with environmental responsibilities. Congress could, however, enhance its capabilities in the environmental sphere if it created a Congressional Environment Office. Congress should task such an office with (1) responding to the administration's annual state of the environment report, (2) providing analytical help as requested by congressional committees, and (3) preparing environmental impact statements on major bills. The National Environmental Policy Act requires agencies to prepare environmental impact statements, including an analysis of environmental benefits and costs but generally not in the form of formal cost-benefit analysis, in their proposals for legislation and other major actions with a significant impact on the environment.[32] This provision to get the government to look before it leaps has resulted in little looking when it comes to legislation. The problem is, in essence, that the requirement to prepare the impact statement is on the agency, while it is Congress that legislates. Besides, there are so many bills supported in some way by agencies that the task would be overwhelming. Furthermore, there are many other bills not proposed by agencies which therefore fall outside the requirements of the statute.

There is no practical way to prepare environmental impact statements on all bills that would have a significant impact on the environment. Consequently, we are not talking about a blanket requirement or one that would be enforceable in court. Rather, we suggest that Congress task the director of the Congressional Environment Office to choose which bills to analyze on the basis of (a) their likelihood of passage, (b) the magnitude of their impact on the environment, and (c) the likelihood that an impact statement would inform public understanding.

Recommendations on Decision Making

Establish expert proposal systems to develop win-win solutions to the logjam:

- The administration and Congress should establish systems through which panels of experts can propose environmental legislation to Congress to help it cope with the complexity of environmental legislation. These panels should be modeled on the panels of the National Academy of Sciences. Alternatively, agencies could be tasked to propose legislation.

Improve agency science and broaden expert participation in rulemaking:

- Agencies should make it easier for experts to participate in rulemaking by requiring agencies to specify questions to elicit the experts' knowledge. Agencies also should use the Internet to enable experts to collaboratively evaluate each other's answers to these questions.
- Congress should require environmental agencies to establish groups of outside scientific advisers to help agencies improve their assessments of environmental harms and methods for their reduction.

  These groups should be involved early in the science assessment process and work with stakeholders in the agency, those regulated, and environmental groups from the beginning of a regulatory process to assess environmental harms and the feasibility and attributes of alternative regulatory tools and the means to reduce these harms.

Promote even-handed regulatory impact analysis:

- President Obama should issue a new Executive Order governing the conduct of regulatory impact analysis.
- The new Executive Order should ensure that cost-benefit analysis is used as a neutral analytical tool, that it gives appropriate, balanced weight to all relevant regulatory benefits and costs, and that the data, assumptions, and methodologies underlying cost-benefit analysis are up-to-date.
- The new Executive Order should create a procedure to review an agency's failure to adopt a proposed new regulation.

Promote crosscutting approaches to environmental issues:

- Congress should require the administration to prepare an annual report on the state of the environment.
- Congress should create a Congressional Environment Office.

This chapter's recommendations are aimed specifically at the project's third and fourth principles, but would help achieve the first two by providing intelligent ways to operationalize the new tools and realign responsibility between the federal and state governments. At the same time, some of the recommendations in the previous chapters would advance the third and fourth principles (see Table 3). None of our recommendations are a magic bullet. But together they would make our government smarter at cracking the environmental nut.

Table 3. Summary of Recommendations and the Principles They Further

Principle 1: New Tools
Principle 2: Federal/State Realignment
Principle 3: Trade-offs and Information
Principle 4: Cross-cutting Approaches

Recommendations	Principles			
	New Tools	Federal/ State	Trade-offs	Cross-cutting
Climate change				
Congress should enact a cap-and-trade (or, possibly, a tax) program limiting greenhouse gases: • One program should apply to large stationary sources and fuels; a second should apply to new vehicles. • Energy efficiency labeling and efficiency standards should apply to selected products.	✓	✓	✓	✓
States should be required to adopt energy conservation plans.	✓	✓		✓
Major greenhouse gas sources should be required to report their emissions and large buildings should be required to report their energy usage.	✓			
Air pollution				
When enacting the program to deal with climate change, Congress should also reform the Clean Air Act's framework for regulating conventional air pollution to: • Adopt direct federal controls on all important sources of criteria pollutants that take the form of cap-and-trade programs linked with the program for greenhouse gases. • Require EPA to provide states and localities with guidelines for regulating the small sources of predominantly intrastate pollution left to their control and rank of state and locality performance.	✓	✓	✓	✓

Table 3. *Continued*

Principle 1: New Tools
Principle 2: Federal/State Realignment
Principle 3: Trade-offs and Information
Principle 4: Cross-cutting Approaches

Recommendations	Principles			
	New Tools	Federal/ State	Trade- offs	Cross- cutting
Lands, waters, and other natural resources				
Lands • Congress should require the federal agencies to permanently retire federal land from grazing, if the holder of a grazing permit requests the withdrawal. • Congress should create a commission to propose exchanges of federal land holdings to make them more effective in achieving their purposes. • Congress should authorize assurance of offset credits to farmers and forestry enterprises.	✓	✓	✓	✓
Water pollution • States should be required to develop implementation plans for achieving Total Maximum Daily Loads that specifiy regulatory obligations for point and nonpoint sources. • Agricultural sources covered by state implementation plans should have greater access to farm bill subsidies. • The administration should strongly encourage effluent trading, and Congress should take steps to facilitate such trading.	✓	✓	✓	✓
Oceans • Congress should pass legislation creating an Oceans Zoning Commission to develop legislation for zoning federal ocean waters. • Congress should remove legislative impediments to the the introduction of tradable fisheries permit programs.	✓		✓	✓

Table 3. *Continued*

Principle 1: New Tools
Principle 2: Federal/State Realignment
Principle 3: Trade-offs and Information
Principle 4: Cross-cutting Approaches

Recommendations	Principles			
	New Tools	Federal/State	Trade-offs	Cross-cutting
Smarter government				
Expert proposal systems • The administration and Congress should use panels of experts to propose environmental legislation to Congress.			✓	✓
Agency science and experts • Congress should require environmental agencies to establish groups of outside scientific advisers to help agencies improve their assessments of environmental harms and methods for their reduction. • Agencies should be required to specify questions to elicit experts' knowledge and to use the Internet to enable experts to evaluate each other's responses.			✓	✓
Regulatory impact analysis • The administration should issue a new Executive Order governing the use of regulatory impact analysis that ensures cost-benefit analysis is used as a neutral analytical tool.			✓	✓
Congress should establish a Congressional Environment Office.			✓	✓

CONCLUSION

Tibetan antelope (*Pantholops hodgsoni*), known locally as "chiru." Courtesy of
George B. Schaller.

CHAPTER 8

Breaking the Logjam
"My Antelope"

The Tibetan antelope stands about three feet tall at the shoulder, with reddish-brown flanks and a white underbelly. The male sports slender, caliper-shaped horns up to two feet long. The antelope's soft, dense underfur has helped it survive the harsh winters of the Tibetan Plateau but, ironically, has made it an endangered species. This underfur can be woven into scarves that feel more luxurious than cashmere, yet are so light they can be pulled through a wedding ring. Because such scarves fetch fabulous prices, this fur sells in India for more than one thousand dollars per kilogram. The only way to obtain it is to kill the animals, three to five of which are needed to make a single scarf. Poachers can machine-gun many at a time because the antelope sometimes gather in herds of up to a thousand. The Tibetan antelope is now extinct in some parts of its former range and in another, according to a study, has "declined dramatically (probably due primarily to poaching) from over 2000 estimated in 1991 to only two seen in 1997." The overall population has suffered large declines.[1]

The authority to stop the carnage and extinction lay with the People's Republic of China, which claims to own the Tibetan antelope along with Tibet and the rest of its range. Neither as individuals nor as tribes do Tibetans have a right to the animals. Nonetheless a handful of individuals banded together in the 1990s to protect them. As dramatized in *Mountain Patrol: Kekexili,* an award-winning film distributed by National Geographic, the patrol received some support from the Chinese government but was given neither the rights of an owner nor the power of the police.[2] The patrol was allowed to confiscate antelope hides from poachers and levy fines, both to be turned over to the government, but not permitted to arrest anyone. The government gave the patrol a meager subsidy.

As the film opens, the patrol holds funeral rites for a member murdered by poachers and then sets out in pursuit of the killers. The patrol knows it's on the trail when it finds several hundred antelope carcasses, recently shot, skinned, and left to the birds. These the patrol buries with the same rites as for the murdered colleague. As the pursuit continues, the poachers ambush the patrolmen, killing one and badly wounding another. The patrol's leader, Ri Tai, a quiet, middle-aged man, orders the wounded man taken to the doctor and supplies brought back, but no one has the necessary money. They have received no salary for a year. Ri Tai directs the patrol member charged with carrying out the order to sell the seized hides, which is illegal. It's that or lose the trail.

The patrol meanwhile continues the chase, but before any supplies arrive, one vehicle runs out of gas and another breaks down, so that Ri Tai must leave behind still more colleagues. He is down to one sidekick and only a dozen bullets when he catches up to the top poacher. The villain still has his machine gun and many men. It is Ri Tai who is caught. The poacher asks, "Why have you tried to stop me for all these years?" At this point in a Western, the good guy would pull off fantastic heroics, but this is an "Adult Eastern." Ri Tai responds, "They are my antelope," takes a swing at the villain, and is shot dead.[3]

The cry of "my antelope" resonates with the increasingly shared sense that we, as individuals, must own and exercise personal responsibility for the environment because it is ours. That is certainly what the mountain patrol was doing. The publicity it generated prompted the Chinese government to create a nature preserve and cut poaching to the point that the antelope population has reportedly begun to recover. Yet, few of us would carry our personal responsibility for the environment as far as the mountain patrol did or, for that matter, as far as the film-makers. They too suffered considerable hardships in the high mountains, as movingly recounted on the National Geographic Web site.[4]

Our situation, however, is different from that of the Tibetans. Their government had abdicated responsibility for the environment. Our government is active in promulgating regulations and fielding enforcers. Also, Fortune 500 companies are not machine gun–toting outlaws. Our problem is that the regulations and their enforcement often fail to achieve our environmental goals.

What owning "personal responsibility for the environment" means in our context should include demanding that Congress reform the environmental statutes to incorporate new tools including networks through which government shares with the public the power to find, pick, and carry out solutions. By so doing, Congress can actually demand more of us in terms of results. This book has explained how the federal government can share power in this way with a broad array of private actors as well as state and local governments. These private actors include not only environmental organizations but also, as some examples, firms incentivized to develop and use effective solutions; consumers and investors enabled to demand more of business because of disclosure of their environmental performance; citizens enabled to demand more of state and local government because of clearer lines of responsibility and federally provided information; building owners and residents incentivized by information to improve energy efficiency; and knowledgeable people from outside government finally being given, via the Internet, a meaningful opportunity to bring their expertise to bear on federal regulation.

The financial meltdown is a fresh reminder that we cannot place exclusive reliance on either government or private actors. We need a partnership that combines the best features of both: government, to set objectives, allocate burdens, generate incentives backed up by enforcement, and channel information; and private actors, to find and follow the paths to reach the objectives and hold government accountable. Without governmental goals and monitoring, private greed can thwart public objectives. Without private actors having a considerable role, government will pick ineffective or wasteful measures or go astray. Given the complexities of the environmental problems and of our society and economy, hierarchical regulation from Washington cannot dictate the inventions and adaptations needed to protect the environment and enhance prosperity. Besides, all too often, public officials acting in the name of protecting the environment have used hierarchical regulation to dictate actions that harmed the environment and the public in order to grant economic rewards to allied interest groups.[5] Still another virtue of involving more people in environmental protection is that there will be more pressure on Congress to keep adapting environmental statutes to changes in circumstance and knowledge.

New statutes are needed to bring the new network tools to bear on problems for which the old hierarchical form of regulation has proven insufficient. Agencies have, to their credit, tried to portage around the legislative logjam, but the statutes limit their ability to do so.[6] Thus, it is essential that Congress pass new statutes that allow the use of network tools needed to solve problems and, in some cases, waive mandates to use old tools; the incentives and the necessary latitude provided by the new tools will be of little use if the old tools obstruct their work.

The new tools will not only vindicate the first of the four principles upon which this book and our project are based but also help realize the other three. To implement the old hierarchical tools, Congress had to conscript the states to help the federal regulators, but at the considerable price of lengthening and complicating the chain of command. With network tools, however, Congress can give federal regulators direct control of the sources requiring national attention. This in turn provides an impetus for Congress to grant states the primary role in dealing with the remaining sources. As it is, federal agencies are given more duties than they can discharge with the resources that Congress provides. This shortage will get worse as climate change demands increasing attention and the downturn in the economy puts the federal budget under increasing strain.

The network tools will also prompt Congress to face the hard choices between competing objectives. Our institutional reforms will provide Congress with reliable information upon which to base its decisions. This vindicates our third principle. In contrast, the current statutes all too often force agencies to hide the inevitable trade-offs. This is bad government.

Finally, the network tools make it easier to see the crosscutting nature of environmental problems, and institutional reforms provide information on them, thus implementing our fourth principle. In contrast, existing statutes take a compartmentalized approach that leads to fragmented and myopic measures that are too often inconsistent and ineffective.

From all this, it might seem that the legislators in Congress fail to appreciate their constituents' concerns for environmental quality and for achieving it without pointless waste. The problem is not, however, the legislators but the institution in which they serve, Congress. Its very name suggests the coming together of diverse points of view and the finding of the common ground necessary to move forward. But the momentum Congress achieved in the 1970s through bipartisan environmental statutes has succumbed to three decades of trench warfare fuelled by wedge politics.[7] The upshot is the logjam.

Can the logjam be broken? In the hope that a window of opportunity would open when a new Congress and a new administration took office in 2009, we launched a project in 2006 to prepare for them with a comprehensive set of concrete ideas for reforming the environmental statutes. We did so with the conviction that ideas matter, and not just in China, where an idea about the peril to the Tibetan antelope led to steps to save it. In the United States, the idea that citizens should know the risks in their neighborhood produced the legislation establishing the Toxics Release Inventory that in turn catalyzed big decreases in toxic emissions.[8]

The ideas that are most important for breaking the logjam are those that produce the most environmental gain for the least economic pain. It is these that are most apt to make it through the legislative process. Such an idea was the cap-and-trade program for acid rain. By producing more with less, it eased the regional and partisan strains that had held up action for so long.[9] Our project has focused on such ideas.

Moreover, we have developed these ideas with an eye to the most critical concerns of key participants in environmental protection. Environmental groups have been understandably concerned that new legislation would weaken the hard-won gains achieved under old statutes. But we should not be satisfied to keep the old statutes just because they have made large gains in the past and continue to make some gains, at the price, however, of increasing complexity and cost. As Paul Portney, former president of Resources for the Future and now dean of the business school at the University of Arizona, told the project's symposium, "The good has become the enemy of the better."[10] Our proposals would use the efficiencies yielded by smarter tools to produce better environmental quality than could be achieved under the old statutes, and at lower cost.

Business interests have, for their part, been understandably concerned that new legislation could give the agencies expanded powers with little meaningful guidance—a blank check to regulate. Our proposals would have Congress write into the statutes how much is to be done and how to allocate the burden. Congress can enact such statutes, despite the limits on its time and knowledge, if it uses network tools that simplify the basic choices to be made and calls on help through the expert proposal systems that we advocate.

These proposals place a burden on Congress to take responsibility and make fundamental structural changes, but counterintuitively, that will be easier than trying to recalibrate existing statutes often framed with the stated objective of protecting the environment without facing up to, or even acknowledging, the hard choices that must be made in actually achieving that goal while maintaining a productive economy. It is difficult to make progress when the issue is posed at the abstract level of the environment versus the economy. But it is quite possible to do so if new tools, such as those presented in this book, can be used to provide more environmental protection at less cost.

To break the old routines, and the logjams that they have produced, leadership is essential—from the business community, the environmental advocacy community, and Congress, and above all from the president and the public. The executive branch can implement on its own some of the proposals in this book, particularly those in Chapter 7, but most require action by Congress. It is difficult, however, for a body made up of 535 members to change direction, but that is what is required to make environmental protection work in the twenty-first century. To enable Congress to respond to the need, the president must lead. Presidents, of course, face many other problems, including the economy, but how we go about protecting the environment is critical to the economy also. To lead successfully, the president needs the understanding and support of the public. That is why we wrote this book.

Notes

Chapter 1. Coping with Complexity

1. Although the statute seeks to provide some flexibility, Chapter 5 explains ways in which its effect is generally to the contrary.

2. See, e.g., Clean Water Act, 33 U.S.C. §§ 1251–1387; Comprehensive Environmental Response, Compensation, and Liability Act, 42 U.S.C. §§ 9601–9675; Federal Insecticide, Fungicide, and Rodenticide Act, 7 U.S.C. §§ 136–136y; Safe Drinking Water Act, 42 U.S.C. §§ 300F-300J-26; Solid Waste Disposal Act, 42 U.S.C. §§ 6901–6992k; Toxic Substances Control Act, 15 U.S.C. §§ 2601–2692.

3. See William Ruckelshaus, "Stopping the Pendulum," 12 *Environmental Law Forum* 25, 26 (1995); for EPA, see David Schoenbrod, *Saving Our Environment from Washington: How Congress Grabs Power, Shirks Responsibility, and Shortchanges the People* (New Haven: Yale University Press, 2005), 62–63.

4. Iain D. Couzin & Jens Krause, "Self Organization and Collective Behavior in Vertebrates," 32 *Advances in the Study of Behavior* 1, 1, 2, 21–35 (2003).

5. Iain D. Couzin, "Collective Minds," 445 *Nature* 715 (Feb. 15, 2007).

6. Couzin & Krause, "Self Organization," 29–32 (on perturbations caused by predators).

7. In humans, a "network" is a group of individuals "linked to one another in a way that makes them capable of beneficial cooperation." The individual components must be united by a "standard . . . shared among members of the network to a sufficient degree that they can achieve forms

of reciprocity, exchange, or collective effort"; David Grewal, *Network Power: The Social Dynamics of Globalization* (New Haven: Yale University Press, 2008), 20, 21.

8. The network interaction between the fish "allows them to experience an 'effective range' of perception much larger than their actual [individual] sensory range"; Couzin, "Collective Minds," 715. For the distinction between hierarchies and networks and their attributes, see generally Yaneer Bar-Yam et al., *Making Things Work: Solving Complex Problems in a Complex World* (Cambridge, Mass.: Knowledge Press, 2004).

9. See, e.g., Peter S. Goodman, "Taking Hard New Look at a Greenspan Legacy," *New York Times*, Oct. 9, 2008, sec. A1.

10. Allan R. Gold, "Clean Air Bill: The Question Is, Who Is Picking Up the Check?," *New York Times*, Sept. 17, 1989, sec. A48.

11. Lauraine G. Chestnut & David M. Mills, "A Fresh Look at the Benefits and Costs of the US Acid Rain Program," 77 *Journal of Environmental Management* 252, 252 (2005).

12. The 1990 acid rain legislation is Title IV of the Clean Air Act, 42 U.S.C. §§ 7651–7651o; for reductions in sulfur dioxide emissions, see David Schoenbrod, Joel Schwartz & Ross Sandler, "Air Pollution: Building on the Successes," 17 *New York University Environmental Law Journal* 284, 285 n.5 (2008); for cost savings, see Robert Stavins, "Market-Based Environmental Policies: What Can We Learn from U.S. Experience (and Related Research)?," in Jody Freeman & Charles D. Kolstad, eds., *Moving to Markets in Environmental Regulation: Lessons from Twenty Years of Experience* (New York: Oxford University Press, 2007), 19, 23 (the sulfur dioxide trading program has resulted in "cost savings on the order of $1 billion annually, compared with costs under likely command-and-control regulatory alternatives"). For a detailed ex post discussion of the savings that Phase I of the sulfur dioxide program generated, compared with counterfactual hierarchical policies, see Nathaniel O. Keohane, "Cost Savings from Allowance Trading in the 1990 Clean Air Act: Estimates from a Choice-Based Model," in Freeman & Kolstad, *Moving to Markets*, 194. Empirical evidence about the effects of sulfur dioxide trading in stimulating technological innovation is discussed in Dallas Burtraw, David A. Evans, Alan J. Krupnick, Karen Palmer, and Russel Toth, "Economics of Pollution Trading for SO2 and NOX," 30 Annual Review of Environment and Resources 258, 268–70 (2005); for a more skeptical assessment of the effects on innovation, see David M. Driesen, "Design, Trading, and Innovation," in Freeman & Kolstad, *Moving to Markets*, 436–69. Cap and trade's

environmental and economic advantages are discussed in Richard B. Stewart, "Instrument Choice," in Daniel Bodansky et al., eds., *Oxford Handbook of International Environmental Law* (New York: Oxford University Press, 2007), 147–81. On the number of EPA employees operating the acid rain program, see Sam Napolitano et al., "The U.S. Acid Rain Program: Key Insights from the Design, Operation, and Assessment of a Cap-and-Trade Program," 20 (7) *The Electricity Journal* 47, 55 (Aug./Sept., 2007) (attributing the relatively limited number of employees required to operate the acid rain program partly to its simple and clear rules, which allow EPA to use an integrated information system).

13. As several scholars point out in a recent book, it is important not to characterize environmental statutes as less flexible than they are. See, e.g., Jody Freeman & Charles D. Kolstad, "Prescriptive Environmental Regulations versus Market-Based Incentives," in Freeman & Kolstad, *Moving to Markets* 3, 14; Jason Scott Johnston, "Tradable Pollution Permits and the Regulatory Game," *id.*, 353, 358–64; David M. Driesen, "Design, Trading, and Innovation," *id.*, 436, 447–50. Chapter 5 discusses the degree of control under the Clean Air Act. Some scholars choose to use the term "prescriptive regulation" to describe conventional regulation, rather than command-and-control. See, e.g., Jody Freeman & Charles D. Kolstad, "Prescriptive Environmental Regulations versus Market-Based Incentives," in Freeman & Kolstad, *Moving to Markets*, 5; A. Denny Ellerman, "Are Cap-and-Trade Programs More Environmentally Effective Than Conventional Regulation?," *id.*, 48, 49. We prefer "hierarchical" to "prescriptive" because network approaches necessarily prescribe a norm, but one of quite different character.

14. For the European approach, see A. Denny Ellerman, Barbara K. Buchner & Carlo Carraro, eds., *Allocation in the European Emissions Trading Scheme: Rights, Rents and Fairness* (Cambridge: Cambridge University Press, 2007). The House bill is the American Clean Energy and Security Act of 2009 (ACES Act), H.R. 2454 (2009).

15. See, e.g., Mary Graham, *The Morning After Earth Day: Practical Environmental Politics* (Washington, D.C.: Governance Institute, Brookings Institution Press, 1999), 12–26 (describing changing environmental problems); Daniel J. Fiorino, *The New Environmental Regulation* (Cambridge, Mass.: MIT Press, 2006), 11–12; Cary Coglianese & Jennifer Nash, "Management-Based Strategies: An Emerging Approach to Environmental Protection," in Cary Coglianese & Jennifer Nash, eds., *Leveraging the Private Sector: Management-Based Strategies for Improving*

Environmental Performance (Washington, D.C.: Resources for the Future, 2006), 5–6 (describing contemporary environmental problems).

16. On tight control, see Richard B. Stewart, "A New Generation of Environmental Regulation?," 29 *Capital University Law Review* 21, 27–31 (2001); Schoenbrod, *Saving Our Environment,* ch. 7. For EPA guidance documents, see House Committee on Government Reform, Non-Binding Legal Effect of Agency Guidance Documents, House Report 106–1009, 106th Cong., 2nd sess., 34, 466 (2000).

17. On the dysfunctions of overly specific regulation, see Howard Klee, Jr., & Mahesh Podar, AMOCO/USEPA Pollution Prevention Project: Executive Summary (Amoco & EPA, May 1992); on low-hanging fruit, see Stewart, "A New Generation," 27–32.

18. Ruckelshaus, "Stopping the Pendulum," 28.

19. J. Clarence Davies and Jan Mazurek, *Pollution Control in the United States: Evaluating the System* (Washington, D.C.: Resources for the Future, 1998), 269.

20. Graham, *The Morning After Earth Day,* 90.

21. Fiorino, *The New Environmental Regulation,* ix–x.

22. Marc Allen Eisner, *Governing the Environment: The Transformation of Environmental Regulation* (Boulder: Lynne Rienner Publishers, 2007), 282.

23. On failures of hierarchical regulation, see "A Rising Tide," 388 (8598) *Economist* 97 (Sept. 20, 2008); Peter Schikler, "Has Congress Made It Harder to Save the Fish? An Analysis of the Limited Access Privilege Programs (LAPP) Provisions of the Magnuson-Stevens Fishery Conservation and Management Reauthorization Act of 2006," 17 *New York University Environmental Law Journal* 908, 913–14 (2008). For Festa quote, see Remarks at the Breaking the Logjam Conference, New York University School of Law (March 28, 2008); transcripts of all conference remarks herein cited are available at New York University School of Law.

24. The land area covered by grazing permits is roughly equivalent to the total of the land areas of Maine, New Hampshire, Vermont, New York, Massachusetts, Connecticut, Rhode Island, Pennsylvania, New Jersey, Delaware, Maryland, West Virginia, Virginia, North Carolina, South Carolina, and Georgia. For overgrazing, see John D. Leshy & Molly S. McUsic, "Where's the Beef? Facilitating Voluntary Retirement of Federal Lands from Livestock Grazing," 17 *New York University Environmental Law Journal* 368, 375–77 (2008).

25. On the need for innovation, see Daniel C. Esty, "Breaking the Environmental Law Logjam: The International Dimension," 17 *New York University Environmental Law Journal* 836, 838 (2008). For quotation, see Daniel C. Esty, Remarks at the Breaking the Logjam Conference (March 29, 2008).

26. See Michael P. Vandenbergh & Anne C. Steinmann, "The Carbon-Neutral Individual," 82 *New York University Law Review* 1673 (2007) (discussing how changes in individual behavior could be marshaled to reduce greenhouse gas emissions).

27. Many statutory provisions allow citizens to require agencies to fulfill statutory duties. See, e.g., 42 U.S.C. § 7604. In addition, judicial review of agency regulations has produced other sorts of requirements enforced in court that encumber the agenda. Douglas M. Costle, "Brave New Chemical: The Future Regulatory History of Phlogiston," 33 *Administrative Law Review* 195, 195–201 (1981).

28. Richard J. Lazarus, "The Tragedy of Distrust in the Implementation of Federal Environmental Law," 54 *Law and Contemporary Problems* 311, 323–24 (1991).

29. Bruce A. Ackerman & Richard B. Stewart, "Reforming Environmental Law: The Democratic Case for Market Incentives," 13 *Columbia Journal of Environmental Law* 171 (1988). But see Lisa Heinzerling, "Selling Pollution, Forcing Democracy," 14 *Stanford Environmental Law Journal* 300 (1995).

30. In Chapter 3, we discuss the diversity of scholars who have advocated each of these principles.

31. Indeed, one ex post analysis of Phase I of the acid rain program, which lasted from 1995 to 1999, suggests that "10 percent more abatement" was achieved during this period "than could have been realized by a uniform standard with the same total cost." Keohane, "Cost Savings from Allowance Trading," 196.

Chapter 2. How We Got Lost in Complexity

1. P. M. Driver & D. A. Humphries, *Protean Behavior: The Biology of Unpredictability* (Oxford: Claredon Press, 1988), 47. See also *id.*, 2–3, 35–37, 44–48; Tim Caro, *Antipredator Defenses in Birds and Mammals* (Chicago: University of Chicago Press, 2005), 418, 422.

2. For the burning river, see Jonathan H. Adler, "Fables of the

Cuyahoga: Reconstructing a History of Environmental Protection," 14 *Fordham Environmental Law Journal* 89 (2002); Francis X. Cline, "Navigating the Renaissance of an Ohio River That Once Caught Fire," *New York Times,* Jan. 23, 2000, sec. 1.14. For the offshore oil well, see Richard J. Lazarus, *The Making of Environmental Law* (Chicago: University of Chicago Press, 2004), 59, 75.

3. For dealing with emergencies, see Eugene McQuillan, 6A *The Law of Municipal Corporations* § 24:18 (3rd ed. 2007); for Clean Air Act promise, see 116 *Congressional Record* 42,381 (1970) (remarks of Senator Muskie); for Clean Water Act promise, see 33 U.S.C. § 1251.

4. For Supreme Court quote, see *Train v. NRDC,* 421 U.S. 60, 64 (1975). For a discussion on the structure of the Clean Air Act, see Schoenbrod, *Saving Our Environment,* 27–28. The Clean Water Act and the hazardous waste statute similarly used the combination of mandatory duties, deadlines, and citizen suits to deliver on their promises. E.g., 33 U.S.C. § 1365 (citizen suit provision for water pollution).

5. For bipartisan support, see Lazarus, *Environmental Law,* 69. For congressional and executive motivation, see E. Donald Elliott, Bruce A. Ackerman & John C. Millian, "Toward a Theory of Statutory Evolution: The Federalization of Environmental Law," 1 *Journal of Law, Economics and Organization* 313 (1985). On the complexity of the tasks assigned EPA, see Eisner, *Governing the Environment,* 1–2.

6. Niklas Luhmann, *Law as a Social System* (New York: Oxford University Press, 2004), discusses the limits of hierarchical regulation in dealing with the interdependencies among complex social and economic systems.

7. The literature on old tactics and new threats is discussed in Chapters 1 and 3. For federal environmental legislation, see Lazarus, *Environmental Law,* 125.

8. The "portage" terminology was coined by E. Donald Elliott in "Portage Strategies for Adapting Environmental Law and Policy During the Logjam Era," 17 *New York University Environmental Law Journal* 24 (2008). For Endangered Species Act and flexibility, see J.B. Ruhl, "Endangered Species Act Innovations in the Post-Babbittonian Era—Are There Any?," 14 *Duke Environmental Law & Policy Forum* 419, 430–34 (2004); and John Leshy, "The Babbitt Legacy at the Department of the Interior: A Preliminary View," 31 *Environmental Law* 199, 213–14 (2001). See also Graham, *The Morning After Earth Day,* 99–100 (describing efforts by EPA

to negotiate flexible arrangements with states and industries in 1990s); Eisner, *Governing the Environment*, 93–108 (discussing EPA's reinventing government initiatives during the Clinton era and arguing they were limited by "original regulatory design decisions"). For extension of the cap-and-trade approach, see "Finding of Significant Contribution and Rulemaking for Certain States in the Ozone Transport Assessment Group Region for Purposes of Reducing Regional Transport of Ozone," 63 *Federal Register* 57,356 (Oct. 27, 1998); Clean Air Interstate Rule, Revisions to Acid Rain Program; Revisions to the NOx SIP Call, 70 *Federal Register* 25,162 (May 12, 2005). For court interpretation of the extension, see *North Carolina v. EPA*, 531 F.3d 896 (D.C. Cir. 2008), mandate stayed *North Carolina v. EPA*, 550 F.3d 1176 (D.C. Cir. 2008). The court is of course obligated to uphold what it understands to be the clear meaning of the statute; 5 U.S.C. § 706(2)(C). Whether it read the statute correctly is another question. See Elliott, "Portage Strategies," 25, 45–49, and William F. Pedersen, "Adapting Environmental Law to Global Warming Controls," 17 *New York University Environmental Law Journal* 256, 260 (2008).

9. For Reilly appointment, see Lazarus, *Environmental Law*, 106. For environmentalist criticism of Bush administration, see Lazarus, *Environmental Law*, 126–27. Professor Lazarus notes that, similarly, President Richard Nixon took important environmental actions, felt rebuffed by environmentalists, and came later to take positions supported by business. Lazarus, *Environmental Law*, 126.

10. President Bill Clinton & Vice President Al Gore, "Reinventing Environmental Regulation" (March 16, 1995), at http://govinfo.library.unt.edu/npr/library/rsreport/251a.html.

11. Lazarus, *Environmental Law*, 77, 152.

12. Congress has been plagued by greater polarization along party lines on a host of issues, e.g., Norman J. Ornstein & Thomas E. Mann, *The Broken Branch: How Congress Is Failing America and How to Get It Back on Track* (New York: Oxford University Press, 2006). For congressional unwillingness to compromise, see Elliott, "Portage Strategies," 31; Elliott, Remarks at the Breaking the Logjam Conference (March 28, 2008).

13. Elliott, "Portage Strategies," 33, citing Juliet Eilperin, "Ozone Rules Weakened at Bush's Behest: EPA Scrambles to Justify Action," *Washington Post*, March 14, 2008, sec. A1.

14. Lazarus, *Environmental Law*, 153–56.

15. For Congressional micromanagement, see Schoenbrod, *Saving*

Our Environment, 174–75. For quotation, see Ruckelshaus, "Stopping the Pendulum," 28.

16. On presidential candidates, see Transcript, Barack Obama on "Fox News Sunday" (April 27, 2008), at http://www.foxnews.com/story/0,2933,352785,00.html; James Kanter, "The Trouble with Markets for Carbon," *New York Times* (June 20, 2008), sec. C1 (discussing a market-based approach to climate change by candidates Barack Obama and John McCain). Polls show the public believes that not enough is being to done to protect the environment, and that the public blames our top political leadership more than it blames business. Larry Huntington, Remarks at the First Panel of the Breaking the Logjam Conference (March 28, 2008). See also The Harris Poll, "Global Warming Seen as Problem That Needs to Be Addressed Globally, But Most People Want US to Take the Lead," (Nov. 7, 2007), available at http://www.harrisinteractive.com/harris_poll/index.asp?PID=828.

17. Symposium, "Breaking the Logjam: Environmental Reform for the New Congress and Administration," 17 *New York University Environmental Law Journal* 1 (2008); David Schoenbrod, Richard B. Stewart & Katrina M. Wyman, Project Report (Feb. 2009), and "Climate Change and Air Pollution: An Integrated Proposal," Annex to Project Report (Feb. 2009). These documents are available at the project Web site, www.breakingthelogjam.org.

Chapter 3. Principles of Reform

1. For the beaver as engineer, see Justin P. Wright, Clive G. Jones & Alexander S. Flecker, "An Ecosystem Engineer, the Beaver, Increases Species Richness at the Landscape Scale," 132 *Oecologia* 96 (June 2002), and Dietland Müller-Schwarze & Lixing Sun, *The Beaver: Natural History of a Wetlands Engineer* (Ithaca: Cornell University Press, 2003). For gene changes, see Richard Dawkins, *The Ancestor's Tale: A Pilgrimage to the Dawn of Evolution* (New York: Houghton Mifflin, 2004), 186–91; Müller-Schwarze & Sun, *The Beaver*, 10, 12.

2. Ronald E. Zupko & Robert A. Laures, *Straws in the Wind: Medieval Urban Environmental Law—The Case of Northern Italy* (Boulder: Westview Press, 1996), 1–33. See also Robert M. Alison, "The Earliest Traces of a Conservation Conscience," 90 *Natural History* 72 (1981).

3. For discussion of changes in the private sector, see, e.g., Eisner, *Governing the Environment*, 133–51 (analyzing corporate environmen-

talism); Daniel C. Esty & Andrew S. Winston, *Green to Gold: How Smart Companies Use Environmental Strategy to Innovate, Create Value, and Build Competitive Advantage* (Hoboken, N.J.: Wiley, 2009); Coglianese & Nash, "Management-Based Strategies," 10–17 (offering examples of the use of management-based strategies in the private sector); Davies & Mazurek, *Pollution Control,* 140–42; Lazarus, *Environmental Law,* 161–65; Fiorino, *The New Environmental Regulation,* 87–98.

4. See, e.g., Felicity Barringer & Andrew Ross Sorkin, "Utility to Limit New Coal Plants in Big Buyout," *New York Times,* Feb. 25, 2007, sec. 1.1.

5. For "eco kids," see Lisa W. Foderaro, "Pint-Size Eco-Police, Making Parents Proud and Sometimes Crazy," *New York Times,* Oct. 10, 2008, sec. A27. On the significance of green consumerism, see James Gustave Speth, *The Bridge at the Edge of the World: Capitalism, the Environment, and Crossing from Crisis to Sustainability* (New Haven: Yale University Press, 2008), 149–56. But see Eisner, *Governing the Environment,* 134–35 (questioning its significance).

6. On state success before the Clean Air Act, see Indur Goklany, *Clearing the Air: The Real Story of the War on Air Pollution* (Washington, D.C.: Cato Institute, 1999), 111–14, 132–33, and Joel A. Tarr, *The Search for the Ultimate Sink* (Akron, Ohio: University of Akron Press, 1996), ch. 8. For state action after the Clean Air Act, see Richard Revesz, "Federalism and Environmental Regulation: A Public Choice Analysis," 115 *Harvard Law Review* 553 (2001), and DeWitt John, *Civic Environmentalism: Alternatives to Regulation in States and Communities* (Washington, D.C.: Aspen Institute and National Academy of Public Administration, 1994), xiv; see also Evan J. Ringquist, *Environmental Protection at the State Level: Politics and Progress in Controlling Pollution* (Armonk, N.Y.: Sharpe, 1993), xiii–xiv; Graham, *The Morning After Earth Day,* 70–82. On state action on climate change, see generally Symposium, "Federalism and Climate Change: The Role of the States in a Future Federal Regime," 50 *Arizona Law Review* 673 (2008). On state activity to protect the oceans, see Karen Hansen, Kathryn Mengerink & Michael Sutton, "A Bold New Ocean Agenda: Recommendations for Ocean Governance, Energy Policy, and Health," 39 *Environmental Law Reporter News & Analysis* 10012, 10013 (Jan. 2009).

7. For states' income levels, see Bureau of Economic Analysis, "BEA Archive: Regional Accounts," available at http://www.bea.gov/histdata/RMyear.asp (last visited Sept. 21, 2008). But states vary widely in

resources they devote to environmental protection. See Graham, *The Morning After Earth Day*, 81; National Academy of Public Administration, *Setting Priorities, Getting Results: A New Direction for EPA* (Washington, D.C.: National Academy of Public Administration, 1995), 74; Davies & Mazurek, *Pollution Control*, 42–43. For public support, see "Bush Criticized as Fear for the Environment Grows," *Los Angeles Times*, April 30, 2001, sec. A1. For early 1970s class divisions, see Mark Z. Barabak "The Rise of Anti-Ecology," *Time*, Aug. 3, 1970, 42. For NRDC membership, see Natural Resources Defense Council, "About Us," available at http://www.nrdc.org/about/ (downloaded Nov. 14, 2008). For state and local groups, see Robert Lichter & Stanley Rothman, *Environmental Cancer: A Political Disease?* (New Haven: Yale University Press, 1999), 26.

8. Ruckelshaus, "Stopping the Pendulum," 28.

9. On the history of ideas for pollution taxes and cap and trade, see Lisa Heinzerling, "Selling Pollution, Forcing Democracy," 14 *Stanford Environmental Law Journal* 300, 305–11 (1995).

10. Chapter 5 further discusses the differences between cap and trade and hierarchical regulation.

11. Grewal, *Network Power*, 20–21 (explaining uniting power of standards).

12. See Chapter 1, n. 12, on effects of sulfur dioxide trading on technological innovation.

13. See Chapter 1, n. 31.

14. Some cap-and-trade programs have been undermined by government granting an excessive amount of allowances so that they total more than the cap. This can be prevented with a provision that ratchets back the allowances pro rata so that their total does not exceed the cap. See Lesley K. McAllister, "The Over Allocation Problem in Cap-and-Trade: Moving Towards Stringency," 34 *Columbia Journal of Environmental Law* 395 (2009). For penalties, see Napolitano et al., "Acid Rain Program," 49, 58n.7.

15. For description of continuous emission monitors, see National Research Council of the National Academies, *Air Quality Management in the United States* (Washington, D.C.: National Academies Press, 2004), 194. For monitoring acid rain program, see National Research Council, *Air Quality Management*, 97. For need for improvements in monitoring capability, National Research Council, *Air Quality Management*, 194–95, 215, 286–87. For estimation of emissions, as William Pedersen shows,

the same level of accuracy need not be required for smaller sources. See Pedersen, "Adapting Environmental Law," 264–65.

16. For chance of hot spots, see National Research Council, *Air Quality Management*, 205–6. For safeguards, see National Research Council, *Air Quality Management*, 206–7.

17. Credit/offset, like cap and trading, rewards firms that can reduce pollution most readily to shoulder more of the burden and incentivizes all firms to reduce their reduction costs. By saving cost and providing flexibility, a credit/offset trading system made it possible to accelerate the phase down in the lead content of leaded gasoline in the 1980s. On the lead trading program, see Richard G. Newell & Kristian Rogers, "The Market-Based Lead Phasedown," in Freeman & Kolstad, *Moving to Markets*, 171–93.

18. For environmental pricing, see Richard L. Revesz, *Environmental Law and Policy* (New York: Thomson/Foundation Press, 2008), 193. For a database of environmental taxes, fees, and charges in many countries, see Organisation for Economic Co-operation and Development and the European Environmental Agency, OECD/EEA Database on Instruments Used for Environmental Policy and Natural Resources Management, available at http://www2.oecd.org/ecoinst/queries/index.htm. Two Canadian provinces, British Columbia and Quebec, have taxes on carbon. David Duff, "Carbon Taxation in British Columbia," 10 *Vermont Journal of Environmental Law* 87, 90–91 (2008). For congestion pricing, see Maria Newman, "Mayor Proposes a Fee for Driving into Manhattan," *New York Times*, April 22, 2007, available at http://www.nytimes.com/2007/04/22/nyregion/23mayorcnd.html.

19. Emergency Planning and Community Right-to-Know Act of 1986, Pub. L. No. 99–499, 100 Stat. 1728 (1986), codified at 42 U.S.C. 11001; for reporting requirements, see Pub. L. No. 99–499, §§ 311–13, 100 Stat. 1736–47, codified at 42 U.S.C. §§ 11021–23. For community power, see EPA, "What Is the Toxic Release Inventory (TRI) Program," available at http://www.epa.gov/tri/triprogram/whatis.htm (last visited Nov. 22, 2008). For resulting cuts in emissions, see Michael S. Baram, Patricia S. Dillon & Betsy Ruffle, *Managing Chemical Risks: Corporate Response to SARA Title III* (Boca Raton: Lewis Publishers, 1992), 10–11, 40–43; 65 *Federal Register* 24,834, 24,838 (April 27, 2000) ("Nationally, reported TRI emissions have fallen 43 percent since 1988, a time in which industrial production has risen 28 percent. Although other factors

contributed to the decline in emissions, negative press coverage appears to have led some facilities to reduce their TRI emissions"); see also Eisner, *Governing the Environment*, 273; Bradley C. Karkkainen, "Framing Rules: Breaking the Information Bottleneck," 17 *New York University Environmental Law Journal* 75, 89 (2008); Soo-Yeun Lim, "Mandatory Corporate Greenhouse Gas Emissions Disclosure to Encourage Corporate Self-Regulation of Emissions Reduction," 17 *New York University Environmental Law Journal* 854, 856–60 (2008).

20. For smarter regulation, see Speth, *The Bridge at the Edge of the World*. On the impact of informational approaches, see Cary Coglianese, "The Managerial Turn in Environmental Policy," 17 *New York University Environmental Law Journal* 54, 57–58 (2008). See also Cary Coglianese & Jennifer Nash, *Leveraging the Private Sector: Management-Based Strategies for Improving Environmental Performance* (Washington, D.C.: Resources for the Future, 2006), 14–17.

21. For California mandate, see Safe Drinking Water and Toxic Enforcement Act of 1986 ("Proposition 65"), California Health and Safety Code § 25249.5 (1986). For SEC disclosure requirement, see Items 101 (c) (xii) and 103 of Securities and Exchange Commission Regulation S-K, 17 C.F.R. §§ 229.101(c)(xii) and 229.103(5)(2009).

22. For instance, the Forest Stewardship Council, whose establishment was spearheaded by the World Wildlife Fund, certifies forestry operations, as does an industry-competitor organization, the Sustainable Forestry Initiative, which was established by the American Forest and Paper Association. On forest certification, see Benjamin William Cashore, Graeme Auld, and Deanna Newsom, *Governing Through Markets: Forest Certification and the Emergence of Non-State Authority* (New Haven: Yale University Press, 2004); Errol Meidinger, "The Administrative Law of Global Private-Public Regulation: The Case of Forestry," 17 *European Journal of International Law* 47 (2006). The Marine Stewardship Council certifies fish whose purchase is environmentally sound, entitling sellers to so label them to consumers. See Marine Stewardship Council, at http://www.msc.org/. Other eco-labeling regimes are listed in TerraChoice, "The Seven Sins of Greenwashing: Environmental Claims in Consumer Markets, Summary Report: North America" (April 2009), 6. On concerns about eco-labels and greenwashing, see, e.g., Gwendolyn Bounds, "What Do Labels Really Tell You?—As Eco-Seals Proliferate, So Do Doubts," *Wall Street Journal*, April 2, 2009, sec. D1 (referring to Senator Diane Fein-

stein's support for a federal eco-label program to reduce consumer confusion); TerraChoice, "The Seven Sins of Greenwashing," 4–11. For federal "organic" labeling standards, see also Kimberly Ong, "A New Standard: Finding a Way to Go Beyond Organic," 17 *New York University Environmental Law Journal* 883, 907 (2008) (proposing a new independent labeling system for organic foods as well as an organic foods certification system modeled on the the Leadership in Energy and Environmental Design [LEED] green buildings certification system to supplement and go beyond federal organic labeling standards).

23. For a summary of leading climate change bills, see Pew Center, "Climate Action in Congress: U.S. Climate Change Legislation," available at http://www.pewclimate.org/what_s_being_done/in_the_congress.

24. President Bill Clinton & Vice President Al Gore, "Reinventing Environmental Regulation" (March 16, 1995) (Principle 5 of 10 Principles for Reinventing Environmental Protection).

25. Robert Stavins & Bradley Whitehead, "Market-Based Environmental Policies," in Marian R. Chertow & Daniel C. Esty, eds., *Thinking Ecologically: The Next Generation of Environmental Policy* (New Haven: Yale University Press, 1997), 105.

26. National Academy of Public Administration, *environment.gov: Transforming Environmental Protection for the 21st Century* (Washington, D.C.: National Academy of Public Administration, 2000), 14.

27. E. Donald Elliott, "Environmental Markets and Beyond: Three Modest Proposals for the Future of Environmental Law," 29 *Capital University Law Review* 245, 246 (2001).

28. National Research Council, *Air Quality Management*, 196.

29. Eisner, *Governing the Environment*, 277.

30. Transcript, Barack Obama on "Fox News Sunday," Sunday, April 27, 2008, at http://www.foxnews.com/story/0,2933,352785,00.html.

31. See, e.g., Davies & Mazurek, *Pollution Control*, 44; Graham, *The Morning After Earth Day*, 72; National Academy of Public Administration, *Setting Priorities*, 71–72.

32. See, e.g., Schoenbrod, *Saving Our Environment*, 140.

33. On comparing states to the federal government, see, e.g., Richard L. Revesz, "Federalism and Environmental Regulation: A Public Choice Analysis," 115 *Harvard Law Review* 553 (2001). For state environmental successes, see supra, n. 6. For federal preemption of states, see

H.R. Committee on Government Reform, 109th Congress, Minority Staff Special Investigations Division, "Congressional Preemption of State Laws and Regulations" (Committee Print 2006), which found that over the previous five years the House and Senate had passed 73 preemptive provisions, 39 of which became law.

34. President Bill Clinton & Vice President Al Gore, "Reinventing Environmental Regulation" (March 16, 1995).

35. National Academy of Public Administration, *Setting Priorities*, 2.

36. Richard L. Revesz, "Federalism and Interstate Environmental Externalities," 144 *University of Pennsylvania Law Review* 2341, 2415 (1996).

37. Chertow & Esty, *Thinking Ecologically*, 1, 7 (citations removed).

38. Daniel A. Farber, *Eco-Pragmatism: Making Sensible Environmental Decisions in an Uncertain World* (Chicago: University of Chicago Press, 1999), 183.

39. Graham, *The Morning After Earth Day*, 117–18.

40. National Research Council, *Air Quality Management*, 18.

41. Richard B. Stewart, "Pyramids of Sacrifice? Problems of Federalism in Mandating State Implementation of National Environmental Policy," 86 *Yale Law Journal* 1196, 1212 (1977).

42. See Cary Coglianese & Gary E. Marchant, "Shifting Sands: The Limits of Science in Setting Risk Standards," 152 *University of Pennsylvania Law Review* 1255, 1339–47 (2004).

43. Katrina M. Wyman, "Rethinking the ESA to Reflect Human Dominion over Nature," 17 *New York University Environmental Law Journal* 490, 495–96 (2008).

44. For EPA missing deadlines, see Richard J. Lazarus, "The Tragedy of Distrust in the Implementation of Federal Environmental Law," 54 *Law and Contemporary Problems* 311, 323 (1991). For EPA and hazardous air pollutants, see Senate Report No. 101–228, 101st Cong., 1st Sess., 128 (1989) ("EPA has not been willing to write standards so stringent because they would shutdown major segments of American industry."); Farber, *Eco-Pragmatism*, 73; see also Stephen Breyer, *Breaking the Vicious Circle: Toward Effective Risk Regulation* (Cambridge: Harvard University Press, 1995), 12n.86 ("According to John Mendeloff, one of the techniques used by agencies to avoid overregulation is 'refusing to admit that a substance is potentially dangerous because the regulatory consequences of making this admission are so draconian' ").

45. See, e.g., Frank A. Ackerman & Lisa Heinzerling, *Priceless: On*

Knowing the Price of Everything and the Value of Nothing (New York: New Press, 2004); Sidney A. Shapiro & Christopher H. Schroeder, "Beyond Cost-Benefit Analysis: A Pragmatic Reorientation," 32 *Harvard Environmental Law Review* 433, 450–52 (2008).

46. Paul R. Portney, "Air Pollution Policy," in Paul R. Portney, ed., *Public Policies for Environmental Protection* (Washington, D.C.: Resources for the Future, 1990), 27, 88.

47. Breyer, *Breaking the Vicious Circle,* 11 (citations omitted).

48. Marc K. Landy, Marc J. Roberts & Stephen R. Thomas, *The Environmental Protection Agency: Asking the Wrong Questions from Nixon to Clinton* (New York: Oxford University Press, expanded ed., 1994), 321–22.

49. Ruckelshaus, "Stopping the Pendulum," 25, 27.

50. Davies & Mazurek, *Pollution Control,* 281.

51. National Academy of Public Administration, *Setting Priorities,* 3.

52. Robert W. Hahn & Robert E. Litan, *Improving Regulatory Accountability* (Washington, D.C.: American Enterprise Institute for Public Policy Research and The Brookings Institution, 1997), 5.

53. Cass R. Sunstein, *The Cost-Benefit State: The Future of Regulatory Protection* (Chicago: American Bar Association, 2002), 137; Cass R. Sunstein, *Risk and Reason: Safety, Law and the Environment* (New York: Cambridge University Press, 2002), 7.

54. Richard L. Revesz & Michael A. Livermore, *Retaking Rationality: How Cost-Benefit Analysis Can Better Protect the Environment and Our Health* (New York: Oxford University Press, 2008), 3, 12.

55. The EPA was itself created out of a number of separate bureaucratic units in different departments of government. Reorganization Plan No. 3 of 1970, 3 C.F.R. 199 (1970) 84 Stat. 2086 (1970).

56. See, e.g., John D. Graham & Jonathan Baert Wiener, "Confronting Risk Tradeoffs," in John D. Graham & Jonathan Baert Wiener, eds., *Risk Versus Risk: Tradeoffs in Protecting Health and the Environment* (Cambridge: Harvard University Press, 1995), 1, 13 ("The 1977 Clean Air Act requirement that all coal-burning power plants install scrubbers to remove sulfur dioxide from their smokestacks has generated tons of sulfur sludge that must be disposed of elsewhere . . . and has ironically also increased emissions of other pollutants such as the greenhouse gas carbon dioxide because scrubbers reduce energy efficiency, thus requiring extra fuel to be consumed to produce the same amount of electricity.").

57. President Bill Clinton & Vice President Al Gore, "Reinventing Environmental Regulation" (March 16, 1995).

58. Graham & Wiener, "Confronting Risk Tradeoffs," 1, 13.

59. National Academy of Public Administration, *Setting Priorities*, 4.

60. Davies & Mazurek, *Pollution Control*, 288.

61. Graham, *The Morning After Earth Day*, 25–26.

62. Fiorino, *The New Environmental Regulation*, 75.

Chapter 4. Climate Change

1. This book does not address measures to adapt to the effects of climate change or geoengineering to reduce greenhouse gas concentrations in the atmosphere.

2. On the Green River Formation, see James T. Bartis et al., *Oil Shale Development in the United States: Prospects and Policy Issues* (Santa Monica: RAND, 2005), ix. On the amount of recoverable oil, see *id.*, ix (midpoint estimate).

3. For 1949 cost estimate, see Richard H. K. Vietor, *Energy Policy in America Since 1945* (New York: Cambridge University Press, 1984), 55. For OPEC cutting oil exports, see Vietor, *Energy Policy in America*, 46, 47, 187, 193–202, 324. For establishment of Synfuels Corporation, see Pub. L. No. 96–294, 94 Stat. 611 (1980). On the Colony Oil Shale project, see Eliot Marshall, "The Synfuels Shopping List: With the Fading of Commercial Interest in Synfuels, the Federal Government Must Choose from a Variety of Money-losing Concepts," 223 *Science* 31 (Jan. 6, 1984).

4. For termination of Synfuels Corporation, see Pub. L. No. 99–272, 100 Stat. 143 (1986).

5. Oil prices recently dropped from $128.08 per barrel in July 2008 to $35.00 in January 2009. Energy Information Administration, "Summary Statistics: Table 1, Crude Oil Prices (Dollars per Barrel)," *Petroleum Marketing Monthly*, 5, April 2009. For abandoned Parachute Creek project, see Marshall, "The Synfuels Shopping List," 32.

6. For environmental damage, see Bartis et al., *Oil Shale Development*, ch. 5. An alternative technology seeks to extract the energy from the shale without bringing it to the surface and so might have smaller environmental consequences of a conventional sort, though it would still produce large amounts of greenhouse gases; see *id.*, x. For energy use, see *id.*, xii.

7. On air quality and ethanol, see National Research Council, *Air Quality Management*, 160–61. The United Nations Food and Agriculture Organization (FAO) finds that "while biofuels will offset only a modest share of fossil energy use over the next decade, they will have much bigger impacts on agriculture and food security. . . . In many cases, increased emissions from land-use change are likely to offset or even exceed the greenhouse gas savings obtained by replacing fossil fuels with biofuels, and impacts on water, soil and biodiversity are also a concern. Good agricultural practices and increased yields through technological developments and improved infrastructure can help reduce some of these adverse impacts. In the longer run, the emergence of second-generation biofuels may offer additional benefits." Food & Agriculture Organization of the UN, "The State of Food and Agriculture 2008: Biofuels: Prospects, Risks & Opportunities" (Rome, Italy: FAO, 2008), vii. See also, Martha G. Roberts, Timothy D. Male & Theodore P. Toombs, *Potential Impacts of Biofuels Expansion on Natural Resources: A Case Study of the Ogallala Aquifer Region* (New York: Environmental Defense, 2007). For governmental assistance, see "An Ethanol Bailout?: And We Thought We'd Seen Everything," *Wall Street Journal*, Dec. 24, 2008, sec. A10.

8. For the Supreme Court ruling on greenhouse gas emissions, see *Massachusetts v. Environmental Protection Agency*, 549 U.S. 497 (2007). For a lengthy EPA analysis of the consequences of applying the Clean Air Act to greenhouse gases, see "Regulating Greenhouse Gas Emissions Under the Clean Air Act," 73 *Federal Register* 44,354 (July 30, 2008). A report from the Institute for Policy Integrity of NYU School of Law suggests how EPA can best proceed within the confines of the current Clean Air Act. See Inimai M. Chettiar & Jason A Schwartz, *The Road Ahead: EPA's Options and Obligations for Regulating Greenhouse Gases* (New York: Institute for Policy Integrity, April 2009). See also William F. Pederson, "Adapting Environmental Law to Global Warming Controls," 17 *New York University Environmental Law Journal* 256, 269–72 (2008) (describing consequences for New Source Review and Title V operating permits).

9. Although some provisions of the existing statute are compatible with market-based solutions (e.g., the regulation of new vehicles: 42 U.S.C. § 7521[a][6]), Congress should enact special provisions for greenhouse gases to ensure that the market-based solution is as broadly applicable as possible and is not held up by judicial review, let alone being rejected by the courts. We write "in general" because there may be some specific gases or sources not amenable to market-based regulatory solutions that can be reached only through hierarchical regulation.

Leading climate bills in the 110th Congress left greenhouse gases subject to hierarchical regulation under the Clean Air Act. See Lieberman-Warner Climate Security Act of 2008, S. 3036 (2008); Henry Waxman, Safe Climate Act of 2007, H.R. 1590 (2007). However, a proposal by Rick Boucher and John Dingell, Discussion Draft for Climate Change Cap & Trade Program (Oct. 7, 2008), § 301, exempted greenhouse gases from most of the requirements of the Clean Air Act, as does the bill that passed the House in the 111th Congress. The American Clean Energy and Security Act of 2009 (ACES Act), H.R. 2454 (2009). When the legislation would effectively control fossil fuel emissions is analyzed in an email from Michael Wara to Daniel Magraw, June 25, 2009 (on file with the authors).

10. Carolyn Fischer & Richard G. Newell, "Environmental and Technology Policies for Climate Mitigation," Resources for the Future Discussion Paper RFF DP 04–05 (Washington, D.C.: Resources for the Future, Feb. 2007).

11. We take no position on the stringency of the cap, on which there is a vast literature, including William Nordhaus, *A Question of Balance: Weighing the Options on Global Warming Policies* (New Haven: Yale University Press, 2008), ch. 1; Union of Concerned Scientists, *How to Avoid Dangerous Climate Change: A Target for U.S. Emissions Reductions* (Sept. 2007), available at http://www.ucsusa.org/global_warming/solutions/big_picture_solutions/a-target-for-us-emissions.html; Nicholas Herbert Stern, *The Economics of Climate Change: The Stern Review* (New York: Cambridge University Press, 2007). McAllister, "The Over Allocation Problem," makes valuable suggestions on avoiding over-allocation and making the cap more stringent should the costs of achieving the cap be less than expected. On free allowances, see Robert N. Stavins, "Addressing Climate Change with a Comprehensive US Cap-and-Trade System," 24 *Oxford Review of Economic Policy* 298, 314 (2008); Congressional Budget Office, "Trade-Offs in Allocating Allowances for CO_2 Emissions," Economic and Budget Issue Brief (April 25, 2007).

12. "Upstream" is a relative term in that oil, for example, goes from the well to the pipeline, refinery, and on down the stream until its final use. By upstream, we mean somewhere toward the beginning of this stream that is administratively convenient. For passing on cost of allowances, see, e.g., Stavins, "Addressing Climate Change." The most important option for using fossil fuels in ways that do not emit greenhouse

gases is sequestration of carbon from fossil-fueled power plants, which can be encouraged by providing credits.

13. Stavins, "Addressing Climate Change," 314, 318.

14. Regarding other greenhouse gases, some of them are also strato-spheric ozone-destroying chemicals under the Montreal Protocol and should be phased out under it. Under a system of offset credits, sources could receive more credit for a given emission reduction if they verified its amount by quantification methods that were more precise than the baseline default requirements.

15. On state action on climate change, see generally Symposium, "Federalism and Climate Change." Should a state set a cap on sources within the state that is lower than the federal cap on such sources, the state should be allowed to retire the unused federal allowances rather than have them used to increase emissions in other states. For a discussion of such a proposal, see Nicholas Bianco, Jonas Monast, Tim Profeta & Franz Litz, "Allowing States to Retire Allowances Without Affecting National Allowance Prices: A Straw Proposal" (Nicholas Institute for Environmental Policy Solutions, Duke University, and World Resources Institute, March 19, 2009).

16. In particular, the tax should increase over time and apply economy-wide, there should be a separate tax on new vehicles and the carbon content of fuel, and credits should be provided for any emissions or sinks not covered by the tax program.

17. E.g., William D. Nordhaus, "To Tax or Not to Tax: Alternative Approaches to Slowing Global Warming," 1 *Review of Environmental Economics & Policy* 26 (2007); Ian W. H. Parry, "Should We Abandon Cap and Trade in Favor of a CO2 Tax?," 166 *Resources Magazine* 6 (Summer 2007); Ralph Nader & Toby Heaps, "We Need a Global Carbon Tax: The Cap-and-Trade Approach Won't Stop Global Warming," *Wall Street Journal*, Dec. 3, 2008, sec. A17; Kenneth P. Green, Steven F. Hayward & Kevin A. Hassett, "Climate Change: Caps vs. Taxes," Environmental Policy Outlook No. 2 (American Enterprise Institute, June 2007); Richard B. Stewart, "Setting Climate Regulatory Targets in Emissions Trading Regimes," Council on Foreign Relations (2004); Richard B. Stewart & Jonathan B. Wiener, *Reconstructing Climate Policy: Beyond Kyoto* (Washington, D.C.: AEI Press, 2003); Stavins, "Addressing Climate Change."

18. Another problem with a tax is that its environmental performance would be undermined as governments sought to give indirect tax

breaks to their firms to enhance their international competitiveness; it would be very difficult to police such measures.

19. Nordhaus, *A Question of Balance*, 22.

20. Cap and trade or taxes can reduce greenhouse gases at a fraction of the cost of "renewable portfolio standard" and government subsidies for the use of renewable energy sources, according to projections of the impact of these strategies used alone. See Fischer & Newell, "Climate Mitigation," 28–36.

21. To avoid manufacturers having to guess how many vehicles that they would sell, the "cap" should be the carbon footprint of the average vehicle times the number of vehicles produced in the model year rather than some absolute number. In that sense, "cap" might not be quite the right word, but we use the term "cap and trade" because trading would be allowed. New engines not used in vehicles should also be included in this program, with the tax or cap geared to greenhouse gas emissions per unit of work. For CAFE standards, see 49 U.S.C. § 32902.

22. For energy-efficiency labeling requirements, see, e.g., 42 U.S.C. § 6294. For energy-efficiency standards, see, e.g., 42 U.S.C. § 6295.

23. For state energy-efficiency plans, see Pedersen, "Adapting Environmental Law," 277–82. On federal supervision, see Schoenbrod, *Saving Our Environment*, 42–44, 46.

24. See Lim, "Mandatory Corporate Greenhouse Gas Emissions Disclosure."

Chapter 5. Air Pollution

1. Robert E. Leach, "Aging Athletes," in Anthony A. Schepsis & Brian Busconi, eds., *Sports Medicine* (Philadelphia: Lippincott Williams & Wilkins, 2006), 81, 82.

2. The Clean Air Act's enactment and amendments are at Pub. L. No. 91–604, 84 Stat. 1676 (1970); Pub. L. No. 95–95, 91 Stat. 685 (1977); and Pub. L. No. 101–549, 104 Stat. 2399 (1990). The enumeration of duties is based upon the analysis in an email from Iain MacDonald, Research Assistant, NYU School of Law, to David Schoenbrod (July 19, 2009) (on file with authors). It reports that in addition to the 940 uses of "shall" directed against the administrator creating primary duties, there are an additional 512 uses of the word creating subsidiary or implicit duties. In addition it reports 369 uses of the word against others (such as

states or regulated firms), and an additional 161 uses against them creating subsidiary or implicit duties. The email explains the enumeration necessarily required judgment calls and states the criteria used in making them. The page count is based on approximately 420 words per page.

3. See Ruckelshaus, "Stopping the Pendulum," quoted in Davies & Mazurek, *Pollution Control*, 20.

4. For Pedersen, see "Adapting Environmental Law," 260–62. The problem of states revising their state implementation plans (SIPs) to allow sources to increase emissions is more than a theoretical possibility. The Clean Air Interstate Rule (CAIR) would bring about attainment of the ozone and particulate standards within ten years at the outside in most areas. See CAIR, 70 *Federal Register* 25, 162. This prediction was for the old standards, but the new ones are not dramatically different. National Ambient Air Quality Standards for Ozone, 73 *Federal Register* 16,436 (March 27, 2008); Interpretation of the National Ambient Air Quality Standards for PM2.5—Correcting and Simplifying Amendment, 73 *Federal Register* 1,497 (Jan. 9, 2008). Similarly, the caps of the various federal cap-and-trade programs are routinely met. Of course, the state would, in addition to the requirement to attain ambient air-quality standards, still be obligated to limit emissions increases in clean air areas under the Prevention of Significant Deterioration Program. 42 U.S.C. § 7470. Current regulations allow each vehicle manufacturer to average emissions within its fleet as the EPA shows in "Regulating Greenhouse Gas Emissions Under the Clean Air Act," 73 *Federal Register* 44,354, 44,439 (July 30, 2008).

5. See Chapter 3.

6. E.g., National Ambient Air Quality Standards for Lead, 73 *Federal Register* 66,964 (Nov. 12, 2008) (amending NAAQS for lead and setting deadlines for SIPs); National Ambient Air Quality Standards for Ozone, 73 *Federal Register* 16,436 (March 27, 2008); Interpretation of the National Ambient Air Quality Standards for PM2.5—Correcting and Simplifying Amendment, 73 *Federal Register* 1,497 (Jan. 9, 2008).

7. E.g., 42 U.S.C. §7409(a)–(b); 42 U.S.C. §7411(a)(1), 42 U.S.C. §7412(d)(2). Exceptions are permitted only in limited circumstances. 42 U.S.C. §7411(h), 42 U.S.C. §7412(h).

8. Committee on Air Quality Management in the United States, National Research Council, *Air Quality Management in the United States* (National Academies Press, 2004), 176.

9. *Chevron v. NRDC*, 467 U.S. 837 (1984) (reading the statute to permit the EPA in determining whether a facility had had an "emissions increase" that triggered New Source Review, to the emissions of the facility as a whole rather than just the emissions of a new or modified unit, thus allowing the facility to offset the increased emissions from that unit with reductions from existing units).

10. National Research Council, *Air Quality Management*, 215.

11. E.g., *id.*, 188.

12. See e.g., George C. Eads & Michael Fix, *The Reagan Regulatory Strategy* (Washington: Urban Institute Press, 1984), 171–72, discussing an incident where the polluter incorrectly calculated the total emissions of the plant. The difficulties in the traditional bubble reflect many of the complexities of point-source emissions control which make cap and trade preferable. See National Research Council, *Air Quality Management*, 201 (discussing cost-savings in the SO_2 trading scheme), 215 (discussing the limitations of point-source emissions controls).

13. For standards for performance for new stationary sources, see 42 U.S.C. § 7411; 42 U.S.C. § 7475. Such increases from individual plants would typically not be significant in terms of air quality under our proposal, because overall emissions of such a pollutant from all sources would be subject to a declining cap. Under current law, an EPA report found that "credible examples were presented of cases in which uncertainty about the exemption for routine activities has resulted in delay or cancellation of projects which sources say are done for the purpose of maintaining and improving the reliability, efficiency and safety of existing energy capacity." EPA, "New Source Review: Report to the President" (June 2002), 30–31. This passage mentions only one of many potential sources of uncertainty, which are described in Committee on Changes in New Source Review Programs for Stationary Sources of Air Pollution, National Research Council, *New Source Review for Stationary Sources of Air Pollution* (Washington, D.C.: National Academies Press, 2006), ch. 2. For an an empirical examination of the impact of the new and modified source requirement on renovations, see John A. List, Daniel L. Millimet, and W. Warren McHone, "The Unintended Disincentive in the Clean Air Act," 4 Advances in Economic Analysis & Policy 1204 (2004). See also on deterring renovations, Lisa Margonelli, "Waste Not: A Steamy Solution to Global Warming," *Atlantic Monthly*, May 2008, 26.

14. Pedersen, "Adapting Environmental Law," 266–67.

15. For Supreme Court decisions on federal air quality standards,

see *Train v. NRDC,* 421 U.S. 60, 66 (1975); for state implementation plans, see 42 U.S.C. § 7410; for congressional promise to voters, see 116 *Congressional Record* 42,381 (1970) (remarks of Senator Muskie); for violation of NAAQS, see Schoenbrod, *Saving Our Environment,* ch. 5.

16. Schoenbrod, Schwartz & Sandler, "Air Pollution," 284, 285 n.5.

17. *Id.,* 285.

18. National Research Council, *Air Quality Management,* 128.

19. For penalties, see *id.,* 125, 297n.6. It is not uncommon that state implementation plans adopted by states and approved by EPA as adequate to achieve the National Ambient Air Quality Standards are in fact inadequate to do so, according to a thorough study published in 1981; National Commission on Air Quality, *To Breathe Clean Air* (Washington, D.C.: The Commission, 1981), 4, 117. The 2004 National Research Council report suggests much the same. See National Research Council, *Air Quality Management,* 129.

20. The acid rain program used cap and trade; see 42 U.S.C. § 7651. For Clean Air Act and new cars, see Pub. L. No. 91–604, § 202 84 Stat. 1676, 1690 (1970), codified at 42 U.S.C. § 7521(b)(1)(A) (2000). For later regulation of average fleet emissions, see 40 C.F.R. pt. 600 (2009). The programs that dealt with lead in gasoline and ozone-destroying chemicals gave flexibility in other ways, summarized in National Research Council, *Air Quality Management,* 197–98.

21. For 1998 cap-and-trade program, see Finding of Significant Contribution and Rulemaking for Certain States in the Ozone Transport Assessment Group Region for Purposes of Reducing Regional Transport of Ozone, 63 *Federal Register* 57,356 (Oct. 27, 1998), codified at 40 C.F.R. § 51.121 (2009); for 2005 cap-and-trade program, see CAIR, 70 *Federal Register* 25,162.

22. For impediments to trading, see, e.g., 42 U.S.C. §§ 7411, 7412, 7475(a)(4), 7503(a)(1)(B)(2). See also Howard K. Gruenspecht & Robert N. Stavins, "New Source Review Under the Clean Air Act: Ripe for Reform," 147 *Resources Magazine* 19, 20 (Spring 2002).

23. *North Carolina v. EPA,* 531 F.3d 896 (D.C. Cir. 2008) (holding that CAIR conflicts with Clean Air Act); *North Carolina v. EPA,* 550 F.3d 1176 (D.C. Cir. 2008) (remanding to EPA).

24. This proposal follows Pedersen, "Adapting Environmental Law," and Schoenbrod, Schwartz & Sandler, "Air Pollution," in many ways, though it differs from them in critical respects.

25. See 42 U.S.C. § 7550 et seq. (new motor vehicles); § 7671 (household appliances); 42 U.S.C. §§ 7545 (fuels); § 7511b(e) (paints and solvents). See also Schoenbrod, Schwartz & Sandler, "Air Pollution," 300–307.

26. As the National Research Council has recommended, monitoring methods should be developed for additional categories. National Research Council, *Air Quality Management*, 215, 286. In situations where direct monitoring is not feasible for now, emissions might still be estimated with sufficient reliability through surrogate measures. Trading, however, should not be extended to regulation of fuel characteristics essential to make the fuel compatible with emissions-control systems in vehicles.

27. The possibilities include auctioning allowances or giving them away based upon estimates of emissions that would come from reasonably well-controlled sources, as was done with the acid rain program, or starting with current emissions and ratcheting them down.

28. Here, again, we are particularly indebted to Pedersen, "Adapting Environmental Law," 258–62.

29. This safety-valve system would be applicable to any source category subject to trading. On comparative inefficiency of tougher technology-based standards on new and existing sources as a means to reduce emissions over time, see the discussion of New Source Review in Chapter 4.

30. The safety-valve prices would mean that the extent of pollution reduction would be a function not only of the cap picked by Congress in order to achieve the National Ambient Air Quality Standards but also of the level of effort that government wants from industry in moving to achievement of those standards. That is similar to the current Clean Air Act, which varies from region to region the deadlines for achieving the National Ambient Air Quality Standards in light of the relative difficulty of doing so; 42 U.S.C. § 7501.

31. We note, however, that such regulations may call for controls that will also affect, directly or indirectly, emissions of criteria pollutants and/or greenhouse gases from those same sources. Of particular note, regulatory controls on emissions of mercury (an especially hazardous air pollutant) emitted by power plants may also reduce sulfur dioxide emitted by power plants. In that event, there will be a need to coordinate those regulations with criteria pollutant and greenhouse gas regulations for those sources, for the same reasons as discussed above with respect to coordinating criteria pollutant and greenhouse gas regulations; 42 U.S.C. § 7412.

32. EPA's AirData uses the term "point source" rather than "major source." The information in AirData comes from states, and they are supposed to include in the point-source category only major sources, but there appear to be many less significant sources that are reported as point sources. This oddity in AirData is one reason why our proposal on which stationary sources should be subject to federal control is provisional. See "AirData: Access to Air Pollution Data," at http://www.epa.gov/oar/data/index.html. Power plants are in standard industrial classification (SIC) code 4911. "Electric and other services combined" are in SIC 4931. In addition to the twelve categories listed, consideration should also be given to including the largest industrial boilers. For direct federal regulation, see Schoenbrod, Schwartz & Sandler, "Air Pollution," 300.

33. In any event, a more likely way to regulate such sources would be to impose federal requirements on the manufacture of new furnaces and hot-water heaters.

34. EPA does, however, need to improve its emissions inventories, whether the Clean Air Act continues to rely on state implementation plans or, as we recommend, comes to rely primarily on cap and trade for dealing with criteria pollutants.

35. That analysis should also consider the impact of contemplated regulation of mercury under § 112 of the Clean Air Act upon sulfur emissions from power plants; 42 U.S.C. § 7412. See also New Jersey v. EPA, 517 F.3d 574 (D.C. Cir. 2008).

36. Congress included in the statute a requirement that EPA disapprove a state implementation plan if the plan would inflict too much pollution on downwind states but did not provide any guidance for determining how much pollution spillover was too much. Reluctant to arbitrate between contending states, EPA did not take meaningful action under this provision from 1970 until 1998; 42 U.S.C. § 7410(a)(2)(D). Its subsequent response was limited largely to a few pollutants from power plants, and it used a cap-and-trade system. We propose that Congress give EPA more specific guidance for dealing with interstate spillovers. In particular, EPA should be required to impose special emission limits when (1) state-regulated sources in the upwind state contribute more than a statutorily set percentage of a National Ambient Air Quality Standard in a downwind state and (2) the upwind state either (a) imposes a laxer pollution-control regime on the sources near the downwind state or (b) allows emissions from the sources it regulates to exceed emissions allowed by the downwind state by a statutorily set proportion. The idea is

a variation upon a proposal from Thomas W. Merrill, "Golden Rules for Transboundary Pollution," 46 *Duke Law Journal* 931 (1997).

37. For the acid rain trading program, see National Research Council, *Air Quality Management*, 205–6. See also Schoenbrod, Schwartz & Sandler, "Air Pollution," 297–98. This absence of hot spots was not because of sulfur dioxide emissions traded in the acid rain program also being subject to National Ambient Air Quality Standards. These standards did not significantly constrain trading, because ambient concentrations were well below them in most of the country. See Schoenbrod, Schwartz & Sandler, "Air Pollution," 297–98. Some models did, however, predict mercury hot spots from the Clean Air Mercury Rule/Clean Air Interstate Rule programs. For quotation from the NRC on hot spots, see National Research Council, *Air Quality Management*, 206.

38. Baseline emissions could be extracted from existing inventories and made part of the federal permit. We would not apply this requirement to new sources subject to cap and trade because the lower marginal costs of pollution control at new plants would produce a strong incentive to make them especially clean. To produce analogous incentives for new sources in categories not subject to cap and trade, they should be required to purchase offsetting emission reductions from another source.

39. See Chapter 3.

40. See 42 U.S.C. § 7543(b).

41. For Clean Air Act and inspection of light-duty vehicles, see 42 U.S.C. §§ 7511a & 7512a/; for ineffectiveness of inspection requirement, see Committee on Vehicle Emission Inspection and Maintenance Programs, Board on Environmental Studies and Toxicology, Transportation Research Board & National Research Council, *Evaluating Vehicle Emissions Inspection and Maintenance Programs* (Washington, D.C.: National Academies Press, 2001), 2, 4, 43; for recent changes to the requirement, see Schoenbrod, Schwartz & Sandler, "Air Pollution," 309; for eliminating the inspection requirement, see Schoenbrod, Schwartz & Sandler, "Air Pollution," 307.

42. Schoenbrod, Schwartz & Sandler, "Air Pollution," 321.

43. For prevention of significant deterioration, see 42 U.S.C. § 7471; for enhancing visibility, see 42 U.S.C. § 7491 (2000); for current efforts, see John G. Watson, "Visibility Science and Regulation," 52 *Journal of the Air & Waste Management Association* 628, 660 (2002).

44. For New Source Review, see 42 U.S.C. § 7475; 42 U.S.C. § 7503;

for greater reductions with cap and trade, see National Research Council, *New Source Review* (emphasis added), 257.

45. For New Source Performance Standards, see 42 U.S.C. § 7411.

Chapter 6. Lands, Waters, and Other Natural Resources

1. More than a hundred species of ant display army ant behavior; Daniel J. C. Kronauer, "Recent Advances in Army Ant Biology (*Hymenoptera: Formicidae*)," 12 *Myrmecological News* 51, 53 (2008). Some birds specialize in feeding on the creatures that ant armies put into view. *Id.*, 56. For Henry Walter Bates quotation, see *id.*, 51. For collective action, see *id.*, 54.

2. For giving agencies power to decide between competing uses see, e.g., Multiple-Use Sustained-Yield Act of 1960, 16 U.S.C. § 528–31. Regarding interest groups pressuring agencies, this is, of course, an instance of the collective action problem analyzed in Mancur Olson, *The Logic of Collective Action: Public Goods and the Theory of Groups* (Cambridge: Harvard University Press, 1971), 10–11. For organization of grazing interests, see John D. Leshy & Molly S. McUsic, "Where's the Beef? Facilitating Voluntary Retirement of Federal Lands from Livestock Grazing," 17 *New York University Environmental Law Journal* 368, 386 (2008).

3. The entire discussion of grazing rights draws heavily upon Leshy & McUsic, "Livestock Grazing."

4. *Id.*, 386.

5. Not just the Grand Canyon Trust but other preservation groups can afford to purchase permits to stop harm from overgrazing in particularly sensitive areas. *Id.*, 388.

6. Technically speaking, Department of Interior might amend the applicable plan for the lands in question to eliminate the grazing allowed by the permits in question, but only for the limited duration of the plan, and subject to subsequent administrative reversal.

7. Leshy & McUsic, "Livestock Grazing," 388. The retirement would be permanent, subject only to Congress deciding to undo it.

8. Congress can pass a special bill to sanction the retirement of particular grazing permits, but this approach is uncertain and time-consuming and so discourages transactions.

9. See John D. Echeverria, "Regulating Versus Paying Land Owners

to Protect the Environment," 26 *Journal of Land, Resources & Environmental Law* 1, 31 (2005).

10. Elinor Ostrom, *Governing the Commons: The Evolution of Institutions for Collective Action* (New York: Cambridge University Press, 1990).

11. "A Rising Tide," *Economist,* Sept. 20, 2008, 97–98.

12. Christopher Costello, Steven D. Gaines & John Lynham, "Can Catch Shares Prevent Fisheries Collapse?," 321 *Science* 1678 (2008). Tradable catch permits are discussed at Boris Worm et al., "Rebuilding Global Fisheries," 325 *Science* 578, 583 (2009).

13. For tradable permit approach, see Juliet Eilperin, "Study Suggests Sharing the Catch Could Save Fisheries," *Washington Post,* Sept. 22, 2008, sec. A7 (the United States has twelve dedicated access fisheries, "which account for 20 percent of the U.S. fishery's commercial value"). On procedural obstacles, see Peter Schikler, "Has Congress Made It Harder to Save the Fish? An Analysis of the Limited Access Privilege Program (LAPP) Provisions of the Magnuson-Stevens Fishery Conservation and Management Reauthorization Act of 2006," 17 *New York University Environmental Law Journal* 908 (2008). For 2006 legislation, see 16 U.S.C. § 1853a(c)(6) (D); Schikler, "LAPP Provisions," 920.

14. For the Clean Water Act, see Federal Water Pollution Control Act Amendments of 1972, Pub. L. No. 92–500, 86 Stat. 816 et seq., codified at 33 U.S.C. § 1251 et seq. For progress controlling industrial and urban sources, see Jonathan Cannon, "A Bargain for Clean Water," 17 *New York University Environmental Law Journal* 608, 609 (2008). On the regulatory approach EPA has used for point sources, see Cannon, "A Bargain for Clean Water," 618–21. For waters remaining polluted, see Cannon, "A Bargain for Clean Water," 610.

15. For farmers and pollution, see Cannon, "A Bargain for Clean Water," 610. For agricultural nonpoint sources, see G. Tracy Mehan III, "Establishing Markets for Ecological Services: Beyond Water Quality to a Complete Portfolio," 17 *New York University Environmental Law Journal* 638, 639 (2008).

16. For TMDLs, see 33 U.S.C. § 1313(d)(1)(C); see also Cannon, "A Bargain for Clean Water," 623. For states, see 33 U.S.C. § 1313(d)(1)(A), and pt. 130 (2009); see also Cannon, "A Bargain for Clean Water," 622–23. For EPA not requiring state plans, see Cannon, "A Bargain for Clean Water," 623. However, there are states, including Virginia, that require

implementation plans under state law. See Cannon, "A Bargain for Clean Water," 624.

17. Cannon, "A Bargain for Clean Water," 623.

18. To overcome states' reluctance to adopt and enforce state air pollution plans that adequately regulate existing sources, Congress provided that EPA shall require states to impose reasonably available control measures on existing sources in plans for areas that fail to achieve National Ambient Air Quality Standards. 42 U.S.C. §7502(c)(1).

19. On whether EPA requires new legislative authority to require states to develop implementation plans, see Cannon, "A Bargain for Clean Water," 624, stating that EPA "is arguably authorized by the CWA in its present form" to impose such a requirement. For rewarding agricultural operations, see *id.*, 630. For DOA subsidies and TMDLs, see *id.*, 627.

20. For market-based regulation, see *id.*, 631; see also Mehan, "Establishing Markets"; for EPA policy, see, e.g., EPA, "Final Water Quality Trading Policy" (2003), available at http://www.epa.gov/owow/water shed/trading/finalpolicy2003.html. On the limited actual experience with effluent trading, see, e.g., EPA, National Center for Environmental Economics, "The United States Experience with Economic Incentives for Protecting the Environment" (EPA-240-R-01–001, Jan. 2001), 99–106, available at http://yosemite.epa.gov/ee/epa/eerm.nsf/a7a2ee5c6158 cedd852563970080ee30/4336170c9605caf8852569d20076110f ?OpenDocument. For limitation on trading, see Cannon, "A Bargain for Clean Water," 632–33; for absence of binding obligations, see Cannon, "A Bargain for Clean Water," 634; on number of sources to trade among, see Cannon, "A Bargain for Clean Water," 632; on amending the statute, see Cannon, "A Bargain for Clean Water," 633. The requirement that trades be confined to sources that have a fungible impact is an application of the general point that trading schemes must be designed to take due account of the range and quality of service ecosystem services provide. Margaret A. Palmer and Solange Filoso, "Restoration of Ecosystem Services for Environmental Markets," 325 *Science* 575 (2009).

21. Other possibilities for controlling greenhouse gases include granting farmers credits for changes in practices to release less methane. The challenge is both measuring the impact of various practices and determining what practices would have been used in the ordinary course. The latter is a particularly vexing problem. For methodology problems, see Dennis D. Hirsch, "Trading in Ecosystem Services: Carbon Sinks and

the Clean Development Mechanism," 22 *Journal of Land Use and Environmental Law* 632–33 (2007); Nicholas Smallwood, "The Role of U.S. Agriculture in a Comprehensive Greenhouse Gas Emissions Trading Scheme," 17 *New York University Environmental Law Journal* 936, 949 (2008).

22. For combining trading schemes, see J. B. Ruhl, "Agriculture and Ecosystem Services: Strategies for State and Local Governments," 17 *New York University Environmental Law Journal* 424 (2008). For added economic benefits, see generally J.B. Ruhl, Steven E. Kraft & Christopher L. Lant, *The Law and Policy of Ecosystem Services* (Washington, D.C.: Island Press, 2007). For multiple economic rewards, see Barton H. Thompson, Jr., "Ecosystem Services and Natural Capital: Reconceiving Environmental Management," 17 *New York University Environmental Law Journal* 460, 474–85 (2008); Mehan, "Establishing Markets," 644–45.

23. Joshua Eagle, Sarah Newkirk & Barton H. Thompson, Jr., *Taking Stock of the Regional Fishery Management Councils* (Washington, D.C.: Island Press, 2003), 20, 23, 24, 26.

24. Joshua Eagle, James Sanchirico & Barton Thompson, Jr., "Ocean Zoning and Spatial Access Privileges: Rewriting the Tragedy of the Regulated Ocean," 17 *New York University Environmental Law Journal* 646, 663 (2008).

25. Joshua Eagle, "Regional Ocean Governance: The Perils of Multiple-Use Management and the Promise of Agency Diversity," 16 *Duke Environmental Law & Policy Forum* 143, 157–58 (2006). For an alternative approach to zoning, focused on planning California state waters, see Deborah A. Sivas & Margaret R. Caldwell, "A New Vision For California Ocean Governance: Comprehensive Ecosystem-Based Marine Zoning," 27 *Stanford Environmental Law Journal* 209 (2008).

26. See Eagle, Sanchirico & Thompson, "Ocean Zoning," 663.

27. *Id.*, 663–64.

28. For federal land ownership, see George Cameron Coggins, Charles F. Wilkinson, John D. Leshy & Robert L. Fischman, *Federal Public Land and Resources Law*, 6th ed. (New York: Foundation Press, 2007), 12. For federal ownership of western lands, see *id.*

29. For statutory land swaps, see Kai S. Anderson & Deborah Paulus-Jagrič, "A New Land Initiative in Nevada," 17 *New York University Environmental Law Journal* 398 (2008). For examples of small federal lands conveyances, see Omnibus Public Land Management Act of 2009, Pub. L. No. 111–11, § 3305 (conveyance to King and Kittitas Counties

Fire District #51 in Washington State) and § 3302 (conveyance of Elk-horn Cemetery to Jefferson County, Montana).

30. For the first Nevada law concerning land around Las Vegas, see Anderson & Paulus-Jagrič, "A New Land Initiative," 410 (Clark County Conservation of Public Land and Natural Resources Act of 2002); for the second, *id.*, 414 (Lincoln County Conservation, Recreation, and Development Act of 2004); for the third, see White Pine County Conservation, Recreation & Development Act, Title III of the Tax Relief & Health Care Act of 2006, Pub. L. No. 109–432, § 301 et seq., 120 Stat. 2922, 3028.

Chapter 7. Smarter Government

1. Elizabetta Visalberghi et al., "Selection of Effective Stone Tools by Wild Bearded Capuchin Monkeys," 19 (3) *Current Biology* 213 (2009).

2. For environmental regulatory trade-offs, see John E. Blodgett, "Environmental, Health, and Safety Tradeoffs: A Discussion of Policymaking Opportunities and Constraints" (CRS Report RL30043, Feb. 1, 1999); for EPA striking a balance, see 42 U.S.C. §§ 7409(b); 7411(a)(1).

3. But see Lisa Heinzerling, "Selling Pollution Forcing Democracy," 14 *Stanford Environmental Law Journal* 300, 303 (1995).

4. For EPA ducking hard choices on reducing lead in leaded gasoline, see Schoenbrod, *Saving Our Environment*, ch. 4. For EPA and hazardous air pollutants, see David Schoenbrod, "Goals Statutes or Rules Statutes: The Case of the Clean Air Act," 30 *UCLA Law Review* 740, 756, 758–63 (1983) (ascribing failure of EPA to set standards under § 112 for especially hazardous air pollutants to Congress for giving EPA a politically impossible job); Senate Report No. 101–228, 101st Cong., 1st Sess., 128 (1989) ("EPA has not been willing to write standards so stringent because they would shut down major segments of American industry."); see also John P. Dwyer, "The Pathology of Symbolic Legislation," 17 *Ecology Law Quarterly* 233 (1990).

5. For all the length and detail of the Clean Air Act, EPA still has broad discretion on the most important issues: how clean is clean enough and the distribution of the cleanup burden. See Schoenbrod, *Saving Our Environment*, chs. 3–8. Such requirements do, however, facilitate monitoring of the agency's actions by interest groups and influence the agency's choice. Matthew D. McCubbins, Roger G. Noll & Barry R.

Weingast, "Structure and Process, Politics and Policy: Administrative Arrangements and the Political Control of Agencies," 75 *Virginia Law Review* 431 (1989).

6. Examples of agencies invoking science to cloak decisions made on political and policy grounds are discussed in Wendy E. Wagner, "The Science Charade in Toxic Risk Regulation," 95 *Columbia Law Review* 1613 (1995). See also, Landy et al., *Asking the Wrong Questions*, 49–82. For science not dictating results, see Schoenbrod, *Saving Our Environment*, ch. 8. For particulate matter standards, see Coglianese & Marchant, "Shifting Sands," 1265.

7. For a strenuous brief in support of this proposition, see Robert F. Kennedy, Jr., *Crimes Against Nature: How George W. Bush and His Corporate Pals Are Plundering the Country and Hijacking Our Democracy* (New York: HarperCollins, 2004), ch. 5. For report, see Office of Inspector General, Department of the Interior, "Investigative Report: The Endangered Species Act and the Conflict Between Science and Policy (redacted)" (Dec. 10, 2008), available at http://wyden.senate.gov/newsroom/interior_ig_report.pdf.

8. Phil Sharp, Remarks at the Breaking the Logjam Conference (March 28, 2008).

9. E. Donald Elliott, Remarks at the Breaking the Logjam Conference (March 28, 2008).

10. See Elliott, "Portage Strategies," 51–53.

11. See *id.*, 51–52.

12. For legislative consideration, see Stephen Breyer, "The Legislative Veto after *Chadha*," 72 *Georgetown Law Review* 785 (1984). For base closures, see 10 U.S.C. § 2687, Base Closures and Realignments. The statute provides that if the president approves the recommendations, they go into effect unless Congress passes a joint resolution of disapproval. If the proposal was open to an amendment to save a particular base, the interests in favor of keeping the base would be concentrated in the locality around it, while the costs of keeping it open would be diffused among taxpayers nationwide. The bases would therefore be kept open for the same reason that overgrazing of public lands continues.

13. E. Donald Elliott, "Science, Agencies, and the Courts: Is Three a Crowd?," 31 *Environmental Law Reporter* 10125, 10126 (2000).

14. The reviewing court decides whether to vacate the agency rule or leave it in effect while the agency reconsiders it.

15. EPA's Science Advisory Board was created by 42 U.S.C. § 4365 and the Clean Air Scientific Advisory Committee by 42 U.S.C. § 7409(d)(2). The science advisory board process is described in Angus Macbeth & Gary Marchant, "Improving the Government's Environmental Science," 17 *New York University Environmental Law Journal* 134, 162 (2008).

16. See Macbeth & Marchant, "Improving Environmental Science," 159–66.

17. See "What Is the Health Effects Institute?," at http://www.health effects.org/about.htm

18. For the need for systematic assessment, see Revesz & Livermore, *Retaking Rationality*, 15. For producing smart alternatives, see Richard D. Morgenstern, *Economic Analyses at EPA: Assessing Regulatory Impact* (Washington, D.C.: Resources for the Future, 1997), 457, 470–71.

19. Revesz & Livermore, *Retaking Rationality*, 64.

20. Slightly more difficult, but still readily solvable, is monetizing the benefit of nonmarket uses of resources, such as boating on a reservoir.

21. For objections to cost-benefit analysis, see Ackerman & Heinzerling, *Priceless;* Shapiro & Schroeder, "Beyond Cost-Benefit Analysis." For arguments in favor of cost-benefit analysis, see Sunstein, *Risk and Reason.*

22. On weighing risks to human life, see Shapiro & Schroeder, "Beyond Cost-Benefit Analysis," 476–82. For discussion of inevitability of trade-offs, see Chapter 3.

23. See Revesz & Livermore, *Retaking Rationality*, 155.

24. For the argument that current methods are biased against regulation, see Revesz & Livermore, *Retaking Rationality*, 10. For the argument that agencies exaggerate benefits of regulation, see Breyer, in *Breaking the Vicious Circle*, 48–49 (describing a "vicious circle" of factors that lead agencies towards exaggerated risk assessments). For Obama administration review of Executive Order 12866 3 C.F.R. 638 (1993), see Regulatory Review: Memorandum for the Heads of Executive Departments and Agencies, 74 *Federal Register* 5977 (Feb. 3, 2009).

25. On the need for innovation, see Esty, "The International Dimension." For quotation, see Daniel C. Esty, Remarks at the Breaking the Logjam Conference (March 29, 2008).

26. For the Administrative Procedure Act, see Pub. L. No. 79–404, 60 Stat. 237 (1946).

27. Paul R. Verkuil, *Outsourcing Sovereignty: Why Privatization of*

Government Functions Threatens Democracy and What We Can Do About It (Cambridge University Press, 2007), 45–46.

28. The proposals discussed here are based upon an essay by two project participants, Beth S. Noveck & David R. Johnson, "A Complex(ity) Strategy for Breaking the Logjam," 17 *New York University Environmental Law Journal* 170 (2008).

29. Beth Simone Noveck, *Wiki Government: How Technology Can Make Government Better, Democracy Stronger, and Citizens More Powerful* (Washington, D.C.: Brookings Institution, 2009).

30. The Internet should also be used to make environmental information readily available, such as data on emissions of global-warming gases and conventional air pollutants and their effects, as discussed in Chapters 4 and 5. It should also include a wide range of agency guidance and policy documents and studies, as well as applications for environmental permits, as Peter Lehner, executive director of the Natural Resources Defense Council, suggested to our conference. See Peter Lehner, Remarks at the Breaking the Logjam Conference (March 28, 2008); Peter Lehner, "The Logjam: Are Our Environmental Laws Failing Us or Are We Failing Them?," 17 *New York University Environmental Law Journal* 194, 203–4 (2008). This and like data, broken down by source and place, should be put on the Internet in readily searchable form, to help individuals act and organize in their capacity as citizens, consumers, and investors.

31. The last year that CEQ issued an annual report was 1997. EPA took a step in the right direction when in 2008 it issued its Biennial Report on the Environment, available at http://cfpub.epa.gov/ncea/cfm/recordisplay.cfm?deid=190806. It is, however, understandably focused mostly on the strategic goals of EPA rather than on all environmental agencies. Also, it does not make recommendations. Nor is it clear that the reports will be biennial. The 2008 report was the first.

32. For environmental impact statements, see 42 U.S.C. §§ 4332(2)(C).

Chapter 8. Breaking the Logjam

1. The local name for the Tibetan antelope is "chiru." It is in fact not a member of the subfamily Antilopinae but, rather, "most closely related to Caprinae." John Gatesy et al., "A Cladistic Analysis of Mitochondrial Ribosomal DNA from the Bovidae," 7 *Molecular Phylogenetics and Evolution* 303, 317 (1997). For endangered status, see D. P. Mallon & Steven

Charles Kingswood, *Antelopes: Global Survey and Regional Action Plans: Part 4, North Africa, the Middle East and Asia* (Cambridge, U.K.: International Union for Conservation of Nature and Natural Resources, 2001), 174–75. For gathering in herds, see Mallon & Kingswood, *Antelopes: Global Survey,* 174. For partial extinction, see Mallon & Kingswood, *Antelopes: Global Survey,* 174. For declining numbers, see Richard B. Harris, Daniel H. Pletscher, Chris O. Loggers & Daniel J. Miller, "Status and Trends of Tibetan Plateau Mammalian Fauna, Yeniugou, China," 87 *Biological Conservation* 13 (1999), and Mallon & Kingswood, *Antelopes: Global Survey,* 174 ("large decline," "endangered . . . still threatened").

2. *Mountain Patrol: Kekexili,* Columbia Pictures, Huayi Brothers & National Geographic World Films (2006). The National Geographic Web site states the film was "inspired" by real events; http://www.nationalgeo graphic.com/mountainpatrol/.

3. The film is also worth watching for the scenery and the acting, mostly done by locals.

4. Private ownership in the literal sense is far from a panacea for endangered species. One reason is that it would not help where preservation brings no economic substantial gain to the private owner. Nor is it a panacea for many environmental problems such as air pollution. David Schoenbrod, "Unsettled Expectations: Reflections on Four Views of the Common Law and the Environment," in "Symposium on Common Law Environmental Protection," 58 *Case Western Law Review* 863 (2008). There are, however, problems where granting some incidents of private ownership has been useful. See, e.g., Jonathan H. Adler, "Do Conservation Conventions Conserve?," in Julian Morris, ed., *Sustainable Development: Promoting Progress or Perpetuating Poverty* (London: Profile Books, 2002), 15–16. For the hardships of filmmakers, see Teng Jing Shu, "About the Production: A Set-Visit Diary from Journalist Teng Jing Shu," *National Geographic,* available at http://www.nationalgeographic.com/mountain patrol/prod_diary.html.

5. E.g., Bruce A. Ackerman & William T. Hassler, *Clean Coal/Dirty Air: Or How the Clean Air Act Became a Multibillion-Dollar Bail-Out for High-Sulfur Coal Producers and What Should Be Done about It* (New Haven: Yale University Press, 1981) (air pollution regulations designed to benefit eastern coal-mine owners and unions at expense of public). Other examples discussed earlier include corn-based ethanol, in Chapter 4; and grazing permits, in Chapter 1 and Chapter 6.

6. See Chapter 2.

7. Ornstein & Mann, *The Broken Branch.*

8. See Chapter 3.

9. See Chapter 1 (discussing the acid rain program).

10. Paul R. Portney, Remarks at the Breaking the Logjam Conference (March 29, 2008).

Acknowledgments

This book grew out of the project described in the Preface, "Breaking the Logjam: Environmental Reform for the New Congress and Administration." The fifty-plus project participants contributed ideas that proved useful in the writing of this book. Many important insights came from the proposals and critiques that they formally presented at the Breaking the Logjam symposium, from the informal discussions that accompanied it, and from the articles published in the symposium issue of the *New York University Environmental Law Journal*. Collectively, the participants encouraged us to believe that the project was a worthwhile enterprise and contributed substantial intellectual capital.

We called upon some participants for feedback on the draft project report. Phil Sharp arranged and hosted a session at Resources for the Future, and Peter Lehner did likewise at the Natural Resources Defense Council; sessions were also held at the Corporate Environmental Enforcement Council and the American Enterprise Institute, through the kind offices of Steve Hellem and Henry Olsen, respectively. These sessions were the occasion of many important presentations by project members. After the draft report was issued, we held many briefings in Congress and with the new administration. The reactions to the draft and final report helped shape this book.

William Pedersen, in addition to his valuable contributions already acknowledged, provided extremely helpful ongoing counsel on the regulation of climate change and of air pollution, and their interconnection. Kai Anderson, Jonathan Cannon, Joshua Eagle, John Leshy, Molly McUsic, Beth Noveck, and Joel Schwartz provided valuable ongoing advice in their areas of expertise. Ross Sandler read the entire manuscript and gave sage advice.

Iain Couzin, a distinguished expert in collective animal behavior on the faculty of Princeton University, read an early draft of the biological examples found in many of the chapters and made very helpful suggestions.

Carol Casazza Herman, Project Counsel, was integrally involved in planning the project from early on. Her perspectives are reflected not only in the essay she coauthored for the symposium issue but also in this book.

Katherine Schoonover, Project Communications Coordinator, worked with us from the beginning and succeeded in getting every aspect she touched to run smoothly.

Deborah Paulus-Jagrič, Project Reference Librarian, not only provided bibliographic information, coauthored a symposium essay, and provided the illustrations for this book but also made this manuscript respectable in the eyes of various style manuals and prepared the index. She was assisted on some of the illustrations by Regina Chung, graphic designer at New York Law School.

We also learned much from the students in the Environmental Governance Seminar taught at the New York University School of Law in the fall of 2007 and at the New York Law School in the spring of 2009. One of the students in the earlier seminar, Peter Schikler, New York Law School class of 2008, gave of his scientific expertise by suggesting biological examples.

Melissa Witte, New York Law School class of 2009, provided excellent research assistance from the initial drafting of this book to its end. She was ably helped at various points by Spencer McCord and Sabrina Steel, also of the New York Law School class of 2009.

James Chapman, NYU Law School LLM 2008, as well as Scott Blair, Alice Byowitz, and Isaac MacDonald of the NYU Law School Class of 2011, provided prompt and cheerful assistance on footnotes.

Katrina Wyman and Richard Stewart particularly wish to acknowledge David Schoenbrod's special role in the "Breaking the Logjam" project. He provided a major impetus for the project, took the lead in drafting the manuscript that became this book, and kept us on track throughout. His energy and enthusiasm were infectious.

Taking on a project of this dimension would have been impossible without funding provided by a donor who wishes to remain anonymous and two New York Law School graduates, Laurence S. Huntington and Louisa Spencer, both of whom have long associations with environmental causes.

Dean Richard Matasar of New York Law School, Dean Richard Revesz of New York University School of Law, Christopher Demuth and Arthur Brooks, presidents of the American Enterprise Institute, and their staffs offered full support to our undertaking. We especially wish to single out our assistants, Abigail Haddad, Gemma Jacobs, Rachel Jones, and Basilio Valdehuesa for their help with the project as a whole, with Rachel Jones contributing particularly to this book.

Jean Thomson Black, Executive Editor at Yale University Press, had faith in this project from the beginning and made many useful suggestions. Karen Gangel did a great job of editing the manuscript for the press. Jack Borrebach, production editor at the press, smoothed the way. Our agent, Lynn Chu, of Writers Representatives, could not have done more to look out for our interests.

Last but not least, our families repaid our absences and absent-mindedness with kind suggestions and love.

To each of those who have helped this endeavor, we give a heartfelt thanks.

Index

eco-labeling regimes, 41. *See also* information disclosure; principle 1; principle 3
ecosystem services, 53, 109, 116
effluent trading, 107–8, 115
Eisner, Marc Allen, 12, 42
election 2008, 28
Elliott, E. Donald, 26, 42, 122–23, 124
emissions allowances, trading of. *See* cap and trade
emissions from new vehicles, 83, 85, 87, 90
emissions monitoring, 38
Endangered Species Act, 23, 49
energy conservation subsidies, 67–68
energy efficiency. *See* information disclosure
energy efficiency plans, state, 69–70, 71, 95. *See also* GHG regulation; principle 2
energy efficiency standards, 68–69
Ensign, John, 113
environmental agencies, federal, 26, 44, 52. *See also* agencies, federal
environmental awareness, new, 34
environmental challenges, ix–x, 10–11, 20, 21, 35
Environmental Defense Fund, xiii, 4, 13
environmental fees, 39
environmental groups, 34, 35, 132
environmental impact statements, 136
environmental laws, federal: hierarchical methods of, 3–4, 9, 10–11; and network tools, 9, 15–17; and new environmental challenges, 10–11 (*see also* climate change; GHG regulation); obsolescence of, 20, 25; legislative logjam since 1990, 22–23, 26; from 1970 to present (table), 24; partisan divide on, 26–27. *See also* Clean Air Act; Clean Water Act
environmental laws, federal, 1970s: initial successes of, ix; and new environmental challenges, ix–x,

9–11; need for reform, x–xi, 22, 25–26; and new regulatory tools, xi, 16, 35; allocation of federal and state duties, 15, 43–44, 46 (*see also* principle 2); and tradeoffs, 16, 21, 27 (*see also* principle 3); and environmental threats, 1970s, 20; compartmentalization, 21, 52–53 (*see also* principle 4); duties imposed by, 21; expectations for, 22, 82; difficulty updating, 25–26, 27–28; and states, conscription of, 43. *See also* hierarchical regulation
environmental protection, ix, 23–27, 52–53, 134–36
Environmental Protection Agency: and federal environmental statutes and regulations, 3–4, 11; and hierarchical regulation, 4, 11, 15, 16–17; resources of, 4, 81; cap and trade, 8, 23–25, 38, 42, 85–86; and litigation, 11, 15; and realigning state and federal responsibility, 14–15, 27–28, 46; and state implementation process, complexity of, 15, 44, 83–85; compartmentalization of, 16, 52, 134–35; and cost-benefit analysis, 27, 48, 50–51, 119, 120; and tradeoffs, 48–49, 120, 121, 130; and Clean Air Act, 49, 120; and GHG regulation, 60–61, 70; and state energy efficiency plans, 69–70; administrative burdens on, 89, 91, 121; and Clean Water Act, 105–8; and scientific decision-making, 121, 124–26, 137
environmental quality, public concern for, 14, 28–29, 35
environmental taxes, 39
Esty, Daniel C., 14, 46, 131
ethanol, corn-based, 59–60
European Union, 9, 66, 123
Exclusive Economic Zone, 110–11, 114
experts' participation in rulemaking. *See under* agencies, federal